ABOUT GRIEF

ABOUT GRIEF

Insights, Setbacks, Grace Notes, Taboos

RON MARASCO and BRIAN SHUFF

Ivan R. Dee

CHICAGO

ABOUT GRIEF. Copyright © 2010 by Ron Marasco and Brian Shuff. All rights reserved, including the right to reproduce this book or portions thereof in any form. For information, address: Ivan R. Dee, Publisher, 1332 North Halsted Street, Chicago 60642, a member of the Rowman & Littlefield Publishing Group. Manufactured in the United States of America and printed on acid-free paper.

www.ivanrdee.com

Library of Congress Cataloging-in-Publication Data:
Marasco, Ron.
About grief : insights, setbacks, grace notes, taboos / Ron Marasco
and Brian Shuff.
p. cm.
ISBN 978-1-56663-858-6 (cloth : alk. paper)
1. Grief. 2. Bereavement—Psychological aspects. 3. Counseling.
I. Shuff, Brian. II. Title.
BF575.G7.M35 2010
155.9'37—dc22   2010015069

For David Shuff

CONTENTS

ABOUT GRIEF

A BOOK ABOUT GRIEF

In the course of writing this book we talked with a great many people. On more than a few occasions we had the same bizarre experience. Someone would ask what we were writing, and we'd say, "We're working on a book about grief." The person's face would immediately brighten with interest, and he or she would say enthusiastically, "A book about *Greece*? How interesting!"

We would then clarify, "No, not Greece, *grief*. We're writing a book about grief." At which point the person's smile would fall and we'd get "the grief look"—a kind of sizing up as to why two people, neither of whom seemed to have dark clouds wafting over their heads, would want to write about grief.

After this initial reaction, though, people would lean forward, intrigued, wanting to know more. Once they saw the coast was clear to actually *talk* about this taboo subject, a flood of thoughts, feelings, questions, and, above all, personal stories poured out of them.

All of this taught us two things. First, there's a market out there for a book on Greece and someone should write it. Second, it taught us something we rediscovered every single day we worked on this project: If you talk about grief openly and honestly, people will talk back.

For most of us, however, this sort of exchange doesn't happen very often. We live in a culture that avoids discussion of this heart-breaking topic. The writer Joan Didion said about Americans, "We don't do grief." It remains a hidden and awkward matter even in a time when few other taboos are left standing.

People will sit on the commuter train reading the most extreme materials, from lurid novels to magazines emblazoned with article titles like "Top Ten Secrets" to doing things you can't believe there are ten ways to do. But if you want to read *On Death and Dying*, it better be wrapped in an old Dan Brown book jacket, or else the conductor may come by and say, "Please put that away, you're depressing the train!"

We don't do grief.

Yet grief still does us. It comes into many of our lives with little or no warning. When it does, we are blindsided, not only by the loss of someone we love but also by how emotionally removed we may become from others. "I feel like I am on an island," said one woman who lost her husband. We heard similar sentiments again and again. This feeling of alienation occurs for those in grief at a time of pain so immense only poets like Caesar Vallejo can describe it:

There are blows in life so hard . . .
Blows as if from something like
God's hate.

Grieving people are in pain *and* on an island—a double whammy that grief, above all other human hurts seems to give.

And there is a reciprocal alienation felt by those *around* people in grief, be they loved ones, friends, acquaintances, or even just the guy at work who passes a grieving person in the hall and has no idea what to say. Let's face it, when it comes to grief, most of us feel like we're "all thumbs." Which is where we hope this book comes in.

The writer C. S. Lewis used to say, "We read to know that we are not alone." While these words may be used to invite anyone to read any book, they are especially apt when picking up a book about grief. That people feel "alone" in the throes of grief is, of course, not a surprise; all grief is about "being left" by someone. But what is surprising, and why we have written this book in the way we have, is how alone people feel when talking about grief and learning about it.

We wanted to help readers learn about grief with the same sense of "breaking the ice" we found in many of our conversations with people. We wanted to help people feel less alone, less intimidated, and less silent about the subject of grief.

If you are grieving, you know how difficult it is to talk with people about what you are experiencing. You worry you'll say something that causes them to react awkwardly. In the movie *Young Frankenstein*, every time a character says the name "Frau Blucher," a team of horses begin neighing. Talking about grief can feel like that—you don't want to scare the horses. So rather than bring up the name of the person who died and hear the neighs, you keep silent, you stay on your island, and this is not as it should be. The goal of this book is to bridge that silence by treating this overwhelming subject in a direct and conversational way.

Toward that end, our book about this difficult subject tries to do three things.

1) Say what people think you shouldn't say in a book about grief.

Often a grieving person would preface a comment to us by saying, "You probably won't want to put this in your book, but . . ."—at which point we couldn't start making notes fast enough. Much of this book calls on these kinds of offhand comments found in conversational asides, in the margins of books, and on late-night walks. In these moments we learned the most—like

how the *death* of someone you love may be the large dramatic
event, but *grief* is the harder slog. As the poet Donald Hall, who
lost his wife, Jane Kenyon, at age forty-six, wrote in a small
poem called "Distressed Haiku":

> You think that their
> dying is the worst
> thing that could happen.

> Then they stay dead.

We learned that grief is what happens after all the drama
ends, when the adrenaline of tragedy has worn off and the in-
laws have gone home and the neighbors have taken back their
cake plates and the "Thank You" notes have been sent and you
stand there saying, "Now what?"

We learned how much managerial detail grieving people
must deal with—including high-maintenance relatives, practi-
cal chores, bills and wills, and "How do I program the TV remote
now that he's gone?"

We learned how often grieving people fail, how they go two
steps forward, eight steps back.

Finally, we learned how often people can, even in the face
of such sadness, be capable of grace notes, those little touches
of humanity that remind us what a rare piece of work human
beings can be and how good life is.

Finally, we learned how people in grief come to know who
they really are. Grief teaches you a lot about yourself.

2) Use plainspoken, humane language.

A great many capable and caring professionals help grieving people. Clinical experts—physicians, psychologists, and
counselors—have much to teach us about the inner workings
of grief. But in many cases their need to maintain professional
credibility keeps them at a distance. Here, for example, is the
writer Sandra Gilbert describing how she was informed of the
sudden and unexpected death of her husband during a surgery.

> The surgeon who came to tell us of my husband's death
> was accompanied by a woman wearing a badge that said
> "Carolyn, Office of Decedent Services"; she carried a large
> folder labeled "Bereavement Packet."

This "Bereavement Packet" language often gets in the way of how people talk about grief. In this book we take a more direct and open-hearted approach; most people in crisis prefer it. When a patient we knew complained to his Oxford-educated oncologist, "Speak English!" the doctor retorted, "I *am* speaking English," to which the patient said, "Then speak American!"

This book is written in "American."

3) Avoid the quasi–New Age infantilizing that often surrounds the subject of grief.

There is plenty of "cute" grief material out there: kitschy teddy bears and Day-Glo balloons and knickknack angels that fly through so much of American grief. (The humorist Paul Rudnick has called angels "Prozac for poor people.") But talking in such a sugary way about this gut-punching subject can alienate a grieving person who is too much of an adult to drink the happy Kool-Aid.

So we adopted these three rules and approached our work as not-very-impartial journalists: mixing observation, research, and our own instincts. We used a variety of sources including movies, plays, print, music, and a few gem books we revisit often. Above all, there are the brave folks who spoke to use about their experience with loss. For sake of privacy we don't use their names but feel they did for the loved ones what the dying Hamlet asks of his friend Horatio: "In this harsh world, draw thy breath in pain to tell my story."

The only people we do mention by name, because their contributions and friendship have meant so much, are Suse and Peter Lowenstein. On December 21, 1988, the Lowensteins' son

Alex, age 21, was flying home to New York with 34 of his class-mates from Syracuse University and 224 other souls when their plane was blown from the sky by Lybian terrorists over Locker-bie, Scotland. This was PanAm Flight 103, and before September 11, 2001, it was the worst-ever terrorist attack upon civilians and a landmark in American grief. Since it happened so near to Christmas, dozens of loved ones were en route to Kennedy Airport in New York for jolly homecomings that didn't happen.

Suse, already a well-respected sculptor, channeled her grief into a multi-piece sculpture that would be fifteen years in the making. She invited anyone who had lost someone on Flight 103 to come to her studio and pose. The pose she asked them to assume was the position their body had taken the moment they heard the news of their loved one's death. Incredibly, seventy-six women volunteered. Although the offer was open to all, no men came.

The work is called *Dark Elegy,* and we were able to see it in Montauk, New York, where the Lowensteins live. These life-size statues are currently on display there for the public, a liv-ing example of a gifted artist and seventy-six women who were willing to draw their breath in pain to tell this harsh world their story.

All the stories and information in this book are here for one reason: to help you realize that you are not the only one. Others out there feel what you feel, even if your feelings are skewed or pathetic or ugly or utterly uncharacteristic of you. Our aim is to make you feel less lonely and, frankly, less nuts.

Grieving people often fear they may be secretly crazy. Like the woman whose husband died young and left her with two small children, aged two and four. It was a great marriage, and he was a great guy. But now he's gone and the wife feels as if he has betrayed her—by getting sick, by dying, by leaving. Naturally she's appalled at herself for feeling this way when she knows full well her husband would have given anything to live. But the woman is, as she expressed it, "Pissed! Pissed! Pissed!" Just imagine her saying such a terrible thing! How irrational! How ungrateful!

How common.

We share this kind of experience so that those who feel the same will know that they, that *you*, are not alone. Singer Dave Matthews can explain a feeling like this, as he did when he spoke to a Los Angeles audience shortly after the death of his friend and bandmate, LeRoi Moore. Matthews told the crowd, "It's always easier to leave than be left." Well put.

This book distills our discoveries into a kind of travelogue through the subject of grief. While it is directed toward someone who is grieving, it has been written with others in mind too, like friends or family members trying to help a loved one who is going through grief. Or people who are merely curious about the subject and wish to shore up their knowledge of this inevitable human experience.

Our book is presented in four chapters, in a progression that is meant to mirror what we found to be the basic trajectory of grieving. Grief begins with the realization of several new "weights" you must now carry. It's like being told you have to haul around a piece of furniture for the rest of your life. The first chapter is called "The Weight of Grief." This chapter details some of what you'll be hauling around.

The griever's struggle then becomes how to process this new weight. The second chapter is called "Processing Honestly." Grief is a heightened time, and at a heightened time it's human nature for people to look around and think, "Gee, I better start acting heightened." Through all the hype one must learn to sort reality from bullshit, because around grief there is plenty of the latter. This chapter identifies some of it.

The third chapter is called "The Nine Consolations." The grieving look for whatever bits of consolation they can find— the faint, brief glimmers of returning joy. The first cartoon *The New Yorker* ran after September 11, 2001, showed a man and a woman sitting in a bar. The man wears a loud sports coat, and the woman says, "I thought I'd never laugh again. And then I saw that jacket." No matter how bottomed out you may feel, little signs can help suggest that your life will go on. This chapter shares the best ones we found.

Finally, the fourth chapter is called "Grief Expressing Itself." Feelings of grief have their own "will" and can come from a place of unknown depth inside you. While most emotional experiences reach only as deep as water, grief seems to hit oil. The feelings that rise to the surface are viscous, flammable, and ancient. These emotions can recur and take you by such surprise that you may find yourself scratching your head and thinking, "What the hell's the matter with me?" This chapter looks at these mysterious upheavals.

The chapters are comprised of small topic essays, each of which can be read in a single sitting of ten minutes or so. That way it's easy to come to a natural stopping point or to say, "What the heck, I'll read one more before I turn off the light."

There are few absolutes in grief, no secret formulas, and not many loopholes. Capturing an experience as personal as griev- ing will always strike a chord with different people in different ways. Everyone must find his or her own path through it; a book can only keep someone company along the way. Because grieving is such an individual experience, as you read you will no doubt contour what we say to fit your unique situation. Please do. That's what this book is for.

CHAPTER ONE

THE WEIGHT OF GRIEF

HEAVY

We begin with a moment from the last scene of Shakespeare's *King Lear*. In Act V the elderly monarch walks on stage carrying his daughter Cordelia, dead in his arms. This is an iconic image of tragic loss, a metaphor for "the weight of grief."

Grief is weight.

The word itself comes from the Middle English *gref*, which meant "heavy." The most common adjective people use in speaking of grief is "unbearable." Grief is something you "bear," a heaviness you learn to carry.

In this scene Lear says a line that is unusual for Shakespeare. It is just one word said over and over again. Five times. The word is "never." The aged king looks down at his daughter's body and, knowing it will have no life in it ever again, says, "Never, never, never, never, never." Lear must say it five times because "never" is such a hard idea to accept.

Grief is the weight of "never," and grieving is the process by which each person says "never"—however many times it takes.

It's different for everyone. Not all deaths cause grief of Lear's weight. Some people lose a loved one and find it, frankly, *bearable*. This in no way reflects their love for the person they have lost. They simply go through the ritual experience of emotion over a loss, and then it's over. We think of this as *mourning* as opposed to the kind of *grief* we are talking about. When asked to define "mourning" as distinct from "grief" we usually say, "Someone 'in mourning' might buy a book on grief, but will probably not get around to reading it."

Grief is different from mourning. Grieving people must read-just their lives to accommodate the new weight of all those "nev-ers" bearing down on them, and they know they have work to do in learning how to carry it all. They *know*. Someone once asked Louis Armstrong for a definition of jazz. He said, "If you have to ask, you'll never know." Grief is the same way. If you have to ask whether or not you have it, you don't. Grief will tell you when it's the real thing.

Not all people who feel grief have experienced a loved one's death. Some people have legitimate feelings of grief over the loss of a relationship, a job, or even a pet. But there are levels of grief, and those kinds of losses are usually replaceable. So don't be one of those people who says to someone who lost a spouse, "This is exactly how I felt when we lost Fluffy." Those who suf-fer a major grief will often encounter people who equate far lesser experiences with theirs, which can be aggravating or alienating or both.

These brief, awkward moments are just a small sample of the many new situations that a grieving person must learn to bear. You'll have many "new normals" to learn about and live with.

Among those "new normals," the biggest one is how many mistakes you will find yourself making. You'll be paying (way overdue) bills and make the check out to the person who has just died instead of to the cable company. You'll come home from grocery shopping, unload your bundles, and put your cell phone in the freezer and the Häagen-Dazs on the counter. You'll go to the mall and forget whether you parked in Structure 3, Level 2, or Structure 2, Level 3, or Structure "damn!," Level "shit!" Frustration with your newfound ineptitude will be the norm.

Grief is also the process by which you learn to accept that you are in grief. Many of the people we spoke with told us how frustrated they were *because* they were grieving, and the toll it was taking on their lives. They were upset because they were so *upset*. This seems like an odd reaction, but it's common. C. S. Lewis, after losing his wife, wrote of this very thing in his seminal work *A Grief Observed*:

> I once read the sentence, "I lay awake all night with a toothache, thinking about toothaches and lying awake." That's true to life. Part of every misery is, so to speak, the misery's shadow or reflection: the fact that you don't merely suffer but have to keep on thinking about the fact that you suffer. I not only live each day in grief, but live each day thinking about living each day in grief.

Although it may be hard to get around, there's no sense suffering over your suffering. Losing a loved one is bad enough. It provides more than enough reasons to feel terrible, so why add to them? Of course this is easy to say, but the feeling may be difficult to escape, so don't be hard on yourself if you feel down *because* you are grieving. It's all part of it.

In grief you face the "new normal" of how people will treat you. You may feel as if you're now going through life with a scarlet "G" emblazoned on your forehead. "Uh-oh! There goes Widow Woman!" And you may find that you are forever ameliorating the many benign tongue-slips of acquaintances. The decorator says: "And over there, can we please replace *that* monstrosity with something better!" You say, "That was one of the vases my Mom painted when she was in the hospice." Then the decorator, who knows that your mother just died, turns purple with embarrassment, and you are stuck with the grievers' lot: feeling bad because someone feels bad because they think they made you feel bad. But part of grief is learning to forgive people for knowing so little about grief. This often entails saying, "They mean well," fully cognizant that this phrase is The International Grieving Person's Code for "They are annoying."

Finally, in grief you learn to carry the weight of a great many bad pictures in your head. The death of a loved one brings with it a barrage of terrible images. Awful tableaus in hospital rooms, the looks on people's faces, particular sounds and smells—any number of things your brain decides to take a snapshot of and save forever. The brain is a very good camera with the cruel habit of vividly preserving the images we would most like to forget. This is true no matter how the loved one dies, because even if you don't see it, you imagine it, and the brain can make things worse than they actually are.

The weight of these "new normals," along with countless others that you will surely discover, are what make up grief.

Learning to carry these burdens becomes the task at hand, and one that, for some, takes years, even a lifetime to come to terms with. For others the weight may just be too much. It may literally be unbearable. Isadora Duncan, who lost two of her children in a drowning accident, once said, "There are some sorrows that kill."

It's a stark thing to say, but it's true. It's not so much that sorrow makes someone take his own life, though that obviously happens; what's more common is that grief is allowed to steal someone's "life force." It ends what was best about his or her personality, and turns them into someone whom people write off: "He (or she) was never the same after that."

After losing her partner to a long illness in 2005, the popular poet Mary Oliver wrote about the relationship she once movingly described as "a forty year conversation." Oliver wrote a poem about feeling in the early days of her loss that she simply could not get "any closer" to grief without, herself, dying. But Oliver, as she tells it, indeed "went closer." And, as will likely be true of true, she "did not die."

The name of the poem is "Heavy."

DETAILS

Joan Didion's *The Year of Magical Thinking*, a book about the sudden death of her husband, the writer John Gregory Dunne, is as well written a memoir of individual grief as one is likely to find, and it's been read by millions of people. But the jacket of the book has a touch so subtle that few people have probably noticed it.

It's a simple, dignified jacket without an image. It reads:

Joan Didion
The Year of Magical Thinking

But if you look carefully you'll notice four letters written in a slightly different color:

Joan DidiOn
The Year of Magical THiNking

J-O-H-N. John, the name of her husband. He is there, embedded in the book, even as a faint presence on the jacket.

When you read memoirs of loss or hear stories of grief, you realize how blended lives can become, how hard it can be to tell where one person leaves off and the other begins. A woman told us about her grandfather who had lost his wife of forty years. For all that time, every morning his wife had fixed him a cup of coffee, the only one he drank each day. The morning after she died, he realized that he didn't know exactly how he took his coffee. He knew that for forty years it tasted good, but he wasn't sure how she fixed it. Milk? Whole milk? Skim milk? Half-and-half? One or two spoons of sugar? Equal? Splenda?

Lives become interconnected in the smallest details—cups of coffee. Every relationship is a mix of mutual idiosyncrasies. Real love is not a small blending of big things but a big blending of small things.

Some of these details may, for example, be little expressions that are meaningless to anyone outside the circle of intimacy. Didion's husband used to say to their daughter, Quintana, "I love you more than one more day." Dunne, a screenwriter, took it from an old movie he liked. It was the last thing he said to her as he kissed her goodnight before returning home on the night he died. A few weeks later Quintana was saying those same words at his memorial service.

But the actual words, "I love you more than one more day," are not necessarily what resonate. The line is pretty standard fare for a romantic movie, perhaps even a little corny. What resonates is the shorthand way of speaking that close friends, and especially families, have. Details say so much about a life. Two unrelated people who were familiar with Didion's book found the anecdote about the movie line so touching that each of them, separately, knew the page it appears on (page 68).

Codes and messages and phrases and inside jokes that sound random or even silly to an outsider have deeper meanings for loved ones. In the movie *Broadcast News*, two friends (played by Albert Brooks and Holly Hunter) are making arrangements to get together later in the day. One says to the other, "Okay, I'll meet you at the place near the thing where we went that time." The other immediately nods in agreement. What could be clearer—between friends?

Edith Wharton, the first woman to win the Pulitzer Prize for fiction, said this of humor's role between people:

> The real marriage of true minds is for any two people to possess a sense of humor or irony pitched in exactly the same key, so that their joint glances at any subject cross like interarching lights.

When a loved one dies, someone with whom you've shared this "marriage of true minds," the funny stuff can be terrible to lose.

An example of this "inner-circle shorthand" came to us from two sisters. When they talked about their control-freak, high-maintenance mother, they always used the name "Lana," even though this was not her real name. When we asked why they called her "Lana," they said, "It's 'anal' spelled backward."

Families are filled with these kinds of funny details. The joke grandpa tells every Christmas Eve that everyone else knows word for word. The year Nana forgot to turn the oven on and the whole family sat around for hours wondering why the ham wasn't done. Which cousins to avoid talking politics with at all costs after last year's donnybrook. These jokes and stories are the stuff of family gatherings for years, usually with the main character frantically trying to defend himself. "I didn't throw the fork at Aunt Minnie! I was *gesturing,* and it slipped out of my hand!"

But these intimate connections extend beyond humor. Think of your own version of any of these details—phrases said to good-night kisses, shorthand landmarks, nicknames, dinner dynamics, can't-wait-to-tell-you laughs, unique languages spoken by only two, or three, or five. Details people share. When death comes, it rips many of these details from the life of the survivor.

The details are so hard to lose because they verify how much you loved someone. The people you love most are the people about whom you know the most details.

Joan Didion's book brims with details about her husband. We learn what scotch he drank, what books he read, what kind of shirts he wore (Brooks Brothers), what he carried in his pocket (money clip with credit cards, no wallet), the route of his habitual morning walk, the haunts he dined at in New York and Los Angeles. But as the writer Marianne Wiggins points out, Didion never once uses the word "love" in referring to her husband. "She never writes, 'I loved him.' Never writes, 'He loved me.' But their love, in all its imperfections, is there page after page." It's in the details.

After a loved one dies, the most painful details to lose are the smallest, most banal you can imagine. This is because the things that are most familiar, most "everyday," embed themselves deepest in the fabric of our lives. In the words of the novelist James Salter:

> Life is meals. Life is weather. Lunch on a blue checkered
> cloth on which salt has been spilled. The smell of tobacco.
> Brie, yellow apples, wood-handled knives.

Life is the little things, the everyday things. When Donald Hall's wife died of cancer, he said, "If anyone had asked Jane and me, 'Which was the best year of your lives together?' we could have agreed on an answer: 'The one we remember least.'" Hall and Kenyon most cherished "a day of quiet and work," those forgettable hours filled with what C. S. Lewis called the "heartbreaking commonplace." It's this commonplace stuff, the "yellow apples" of life, that break your heart more than the drama of a death.

A happily married man came home from work one day and found his wife who had died very suddenly. Because she died inside their home, most people, including the man himself,

assumed he would sell the house and move away. The trau-
matic image of finding his wife there would be too much to
handle. But in the days after his wife's death he began to realize
that he felt okay being in the house. A few weeks later he went
back to work, and for a while everything was fine.

Then one day, as he was driving home, something happened.
Their house was on the corner of a busy road, and the man was
stopped at a red light, waiting to make a left turn onto his street
and into his driveway. It was the first time he had encountered a
red light at that intersection since returning to work. He realized
how in all the years he'd been commuting, every time he got a
red light at that intersection he'd spend the waiting time looking
at his wife, whom he could see through their kitchen window
as she prepared dinner. Waiting at that red light, on that day,
he realized he would have to sell the house. Coming home and
finding his wife dead in the house could be managed, but an
empty kitchen window was too much to bear.

Life is details, and grief wrenches them away.

When death cuts away the details, in their place it leaves not
so much a void but the discernible weight of *pain* to fill in the
holes. Pain is a definite presence; it fills a room. We don't say "I
have pain in me," we say, "I'm *in* pain," because when you're in
pain it feels as big as your whole world. People assume that the
feeling of grief is an absence, but it's actually the overwhelming
presence of pain. A line in an Anne Sexton poem says, "Someone has died, even the trees know it." The pain of grief is a presence that seems to permeate even the trees.

In Shakespeare's play *King John*, the character of Constance
speaks about her grief after the death of her young son. It is a
vivid description of the heavy presence of absence.

Grief fills up the room of my absent child,
Lies in his bed, walks up and down with me,

Puts on his pretty looks, repeats his words,
Remembers me of all his gracious parts,
Stuffs out his vacant garment with his form.

This play was written shortly after Shakespeare himself lost a child, his only son, Hamnet. The boy died in 1596. He was eleven.

THE GROUP

Grief always produces a group.

Whether it's people caring for someone who's terminally ill, or dealing with the crisis of a sudden death, or helping someone who's struggling through a major grief, the group is almost always on hand, trying to support the person in need. Sometimes the group is composed of family, sometimes friends, and almost always a mix of both. Consequently there are many "dynamics" at work among them, which is a nice way of saying potential *tension*.

First, there is the issue of what exactly constitutes a family. Seventy-five years ago, people divorced less, and they often lived and died in the same town or even in the same house. But families now find themselves more in a state of flux. We divorce and remarry more, and this can add whole new layers of "relations." We have stepwives, stepchildren, stepdads, stepsisters, stepdogs, stepdentists. At a time of crisis, first marriages and first families become involved or reinvolved. People who haven't seen each other in years, or ever, are suddenly thrown together in a delicate situation.

Friends, too, can be an incredibly varied mix of people. The CEO still has college beer buddies he stays in touch with; the university dean has friends from karate class. Almost everyone has at least one good friend with lots of money and one good friend with very little. When all these people come together, some may vie for status: "I may not have a goddam Ph.D., but I've known him since he was ten!"

Then there is the issue of proximity. While family and friends may live all over the globe, human beings don't die or grieve globally. They do it in small rooms, with whoever is with them. At times of illness and emotional need, nearness matters. But it is often the case that the person who is closest emotionally is not always the closest geographically.

Grief joins together all sorts of people from all sorts of places, at least for a while, as a group. Most are there to support the person in need and to rally 'round the flag of help. But just as flags are rallying points, they have also been known to cause wars. The potential for conflict in the group is great. Ex-wives and old roommates will find themselves in the same room with childhood playmates and uncles, a room that will already be charged with thoughts of mortality, love, religion, what it means to be a friend, and what it means to be family. The delicate balance of group stability wobbles beneath the weight of grief, and sometimes it gives way.

In one episode of *I Love Lucy*, Lucy has a baby. Beforehand, Ricky, Ethel, and Fred practice what they will do when the time comes for Lucy to go to the hospital. They rehearse getting her suitcase, putting on her coat, calling a cab, and whisking her off. But when the real moment comes, they all go nuts. Everyone rushes in different (and wrong) directions, they shout orders and recriminations at one another, and finally Ricky, Ethel, and Fred rush out of the apartment with the suitcase and Lucy's coat (on Fred) to get the cab. Lucy is left staggering around the empty apartment, going into labor, and whimpering, "Hey, wait for me!"

The not-so-funny grief version of this episode happens in many "families."

When it does it usually goes something like this: Everyone begins watching one another, each with his or her own ideas about the "proper" process and procedure for grieving. The atmosphere grows tense and awkward, and no one knows what to say or do. Then, at a moment appropriate or inappropriate, someone thinks he *does* know what to say or do. And he says it. Or does it. Some people tolerate it, others don't. Some people think that the tolerant people are being *too* tolerant, or that the others aren't being tolerant enough. Meanwhile some people will constantly check up on everyone else. And others will analyze the looks and intonations they perceive, and some will begin making lists, because there's always a list maker in every group. Some people will want to smother the people who are most stricken with grief, and others will try to avoid the mess of strong feelings and not deal with any of it. Then the "smotherers" will start a cold war with the "avoiders," which the "avoiders" will want to avoid. Some will suffer openly, others will think these people are trying to monopolize the situation—and in fact some of them *will* be trying to monopolize the situation, because there's always at least one family member who wants the Suffering Medal. All in all, the potential for frustration, anger, and a group dynamic thick with the ooze of bad attitude and heavy with emotional baggage may push the situation into a sinkhole of dysfunction.

So much for "support."

Your group's ability to help you will hinge on whether or not they are in sync with one another. As one psychologist emphasized, "It's important to get everyone on the same page early on." If people are not on the same page, they may be more hindrance than help. Individual members begin working at cross-purposes, tensions mount, the support structure topples, and the very person the group was there to support not only isn't supported but is hurt by the discord.

People may dismiss the person in need, believing he or she is clueless to tensions within the group. They assume that someone who is ill or in deep grief is in too much pain to sense the group's emotional dynamics. But the exact opposite is true. When you are grieving you are unusually sensitive to any emotional wobbles in the family. You are wide open, exposed, hyperaware of the slightest fluctuations in feeling and hypervigilant about trouble on the horizon. Isn't the person who's been in an earthquake the one who is most aware of the slightest intimation of an aftershock? Among the grieving people we spoke with, their experience with group tensions and the ensuing damage to relationships was almost as terrible as the loss itself.

Families who are supporting an ill or grieving member must make many decisions, so there's plenty of opportunity for disagreement. Sometimes a person or faction may become so fixated on "being right" about a point, they miss the fact that the group is breaking apart or the person in need is wandering about, babbling, "Hey, wait for me!"

Yes, it may be worth standing firm on a point, but most of the quarrels we heard of were about the most inconsequential crap. Which caterer to use for the get-together after the funeral? Who's going to ride in what car? Who can stay around a few extra days to help out? These kinds of questions should not be allowed to cause a family support system to splinter. But it happens.

Some of the bad feelings that permeate the emotional air of a group have nothing to do with the situation at hand. They are often the remnants of past resentments and long-standing unexpressed feelings. "You were the star of the football team! I'm gonna be the star of Dad's grief." Or, "My last five girlfriends took advantage of me. I'm not gonna let my siblings do it now." Grief brings plenty of new things to feel, so try not to get caught up with these old wounds.

Most of the chafing that goes on between you and the group will likely stem from poor communication. When you don't tell people your wishes directly, each member of the group is free to "read" your behavior in his or her own way. Grief has a way of turning every loved one into an armchair shrink, so speak your own truth or people will do it for you. The tragic circumstances that bring grief can also be an opportunity for people to communicate more deeply than ever before. Time and again we heard, "It was the first time we stayed up all night just talking," and similar stories.

Another common reason for tension from the group is that people often decide to take action merely for the sake of taking action—Fred putting on Lucy's coat. You often hear the expression "Doing nothing is not an option." But in fact there are plenty of situations where doing nothing is a fine option! This is especially true when it comes to grief.

People tend to be impatient and will want to fix something right away rather than allow nature to take its course. Someone will say, "Mom moped around the house all day! She didn't even fix her hair! We can't let her go on like this!" Truth be told, as long as mom is not boarded up in her room with a bottle of Jack Daniel's and an Uzi, the situation may not need immediate intervention. And she shouldn't be made to feel that there's something wrong with her just because she's very, very sad with her loss.

At times the best thing for the group to do is give you a bit of space. It may be what you need the most. So ask for it.

Company can be a great comfort to a person in grief, but the presence of a group also has unintended consequences. You want to flop on the couch like a zombie, but instead you have to think, "Damn! There aren't clean towels in the guest bathroom." Even too many of those "just checking in" or "wonderin' how you're doin'" phone calls become unwelcome, because "quick calls" turn into emotionally taxing ten-minute conversations.

We heard a funny but revealing story about these types of calls. It happened at the funeral of the wonderful comic actor Dom DeLuise. DeLuise was known for having a large Italian family, and during his funeral one of his beloved sons, while speaking, reminded those in the audience not to forget about their mother Carol—"please make sure to call her." Just then a voice was heard from the audience. It was Carol shouting, "Please don't call me!"

Sometimes the group wants to be attached at the hip to you, but you just want to be left alone. This need for solitude is a part of grieving; it's not meant to be insulting or unappreciative.

Tell people how much you appreciate sitting down and reading the e-mails you get at the end of the day, when things are calm. E-mails and text messages are a better way for people to voice support because they don't have the potential inconvenience of a phone call or "stopping by." You can decide when and how to read them, and whether or not to respond. And it can be comforting to hear a beep-beep, flip open your phone, read "Thinking of U w/love," and hold that thought in your heart without having to give a mini press conference to someone who's calling to talk.

Knowing when they are needed and when they aren't is for the group to determine. Their task, if they wish to do it properly, is to take their cues from you, the person they are ostensibly there to help, and to weigh them against their own instincts. This weighing is difficult, and it's not an exact science. But of all the "group" members we spoke with, we never came across anyone who wasn't trying hard to do right by the person they were there to support. Human and flawed, yes, but they cared and sincerely wished to help. Was there ever any question that Ricky, Ethel, and Fred loved Lucy?

STIGMA

When you grieve you must not only deal with your own emotions but must also handle the often heavy tension in the air between yourself and others. Most people don't know how to act around a grieving person. They don't know what to say, how to say it, or if they should say it. And you will be quite aware of the awkward position others are put in by your mere presence. C. S. Lewis writes:

> An odd by-product of my loss is that I'm aware of being an embarrassment to everyone I meet. At work, at the club, in the street, I see people, as they approach me, trying to make up their minds whether they'll "say something about it" or not. I hate if they do, and if they don't.

These little "should I or shouldn't I" moments can run the gamut from painful to merely awkward.

In some cases people treat the grieving coldly. They go out of their way to avoid bumping into a person they know has lost a loved one. This is especially true if the loss was in some way high profile—as in violence, the death of a child, or a shocking sudden death. As Suse Lowenstein, the woman we spoke about who lost her son on PanAm Flight 103, told us, "People ignore you. They see you coming and turn away before they have to talk with you. I guess they are just too uncomfortable."

This seems like such a weird thing to do—to turn your back on someone in the depths of suffering and grief just to avoid what might be an uncomfortable few minutes. It doesn't make sense. Awkwardness has something to do with it, but there is a deeper reason why many people avoid the bereft.

Joan Didion touches on the reason in the stage adaptation of her book *The Year of Magical Thinking.* The piece is a one-woman show that opened on Broadway starring Vanessa Redgrave in a powerful performance. At one point in the play, Redgrave stares out at the audience and says:

> You think I'm crazy.
> You think I'm crazy because otherwise I'm dangerous.
> Radioactive.
> If I'm sane, what happened to me can happen to you.
> You don't want to hear what I have to tell you.

With her use of the word "radioactive," the distancing and the shunning begin to make sense. People view grief as something dangerous, something toxic, something you don't want to get on you. In the play *Rabbit Hole* there is a line about the loss of a toddler who is killed by a car: "Accidents aren't contagious." But that won't make it hurt any less when you notice an acquaintance avoiding you at the supermarket by pretending to be engrossed in the produce.

Susan Sontag's book *Illness as Metaphor* explores what she calls "metaphoric thinking." This is when people give illness an imaginative context and a value judgment, and turn it into something mythological rather than merely biological. In metaphoric thinking, illness becomes more than just physical cells gone awry; illness is evil, bad luck, punishment, God's judgment, karmic payback for negative thinking. Sontag, who herself struggled for years with cancer, felt this kind of thinking could be psychologically treacherous for a patient, who might internalize all sorts of metaphoric junk and refuse to think clearly about treatment.

A similar kind of "metaphoric" thinking happens around death and grief. Subconsciously we may think that someone who's suffered a tragic loss has been marked by the gods, is in the crosshairs of Fate, has a cloud of darkness hovering over them. We don't want ourselves to be noticed by those same gods, placed in the line of fire by that same Fate, rained on by that same cloud—all of which some people sense will surely happen if they come too close to a grieving person. No one will admit to this, of course. It's so ridiculous, so intellectually indefensible, so immature. We can't even admit to *ourselves* that we think in such irrational terms. But we do.

Often what may look to you like shunning is usually just simple everyday awkwardness. People fumble in particular over what to say. Americans prize "doing" over discussion. When trouble hits and people need help, we roll up our sleeves and get to work. We run marathons, rebuild houses, organize fundraisers, lift sandbags, collect canned goods, wash cars. But when it comes to something less active, like having a quiet conversation on the specifics of grief with someone who hurts, we find this harder.

As difficult as it may be, sometimes people *do* find it in themselves to push through the awkwardness and cross a bridge to someone else's grief.

In the days after the attack on the World Trade Center, the New York City Armory became a makeshift clearinghouse for information about victims. For many, it was the place where they received confirmation that their loved one had perished. It was a scene of wrenching grief. The players from the New York Yankees, who that fall were in a pennant race, were eager to do something, anything, to help the city. A group of them decided to make an impromptu visit to the Armory to be with the families.

But the players were nervous. They knew, as one sportswriter explained, that "most of the people they were set to encounter had either lost loved ones or were holding out hope that their family members would emerge from the disaster five days afterwards."

Yankee manager Joe Torre described arriving at the Armory: "I felt very uncomfortable, like we needed someone to go in and test the waters to see if we had any right being there." Third baseman Scott Brosius said he felt "completely out of place" and kept thinking to himself as he walked into the Armory, "What am *I* doing here? What do *I* have to offer these people."

The scene was tense and awkward.

Then, Torre recalled, "One family looked at us, and their eyes asked us to come closer." All-star outfielder Bernie Williams was the first person to approach someone in the family. Torre said, "I remember Bernie going up to someone and sort of fumbling." Finally Williams blurted out, "I don't know what to say, but you look like you need a hug."

All the players who witnessed the moment said it was the most emotional part of their visit. Not that Bernie Williams hugged someone, because plenty of hugging went on in that Armory. What was so emotional was Williams's blunt admission: "I don't know what to say . . ." To have a strong, able athlete express so candidly how hard it is to reach out to someone in grief changed the whole dynamic. As Torre expressed it, it "broke the ice to see that these people needed this. At that point I realized there was a role for us."

If you've lost a loved one and you see that people are uncomfortable talking to you, you hope they'll just take a deep breath and dive in. You'll be grateful for the honest attempt, however shaky it may be. Tongue-tied-but-genuine beats eloquent-but-saccharine every time. C. S. Lewis said the approach he most admired came from the students at Oxford where he taught:

> I like best the well brought-up young men, almost boys, who walk up to me as if I were a dentist, turn very red, get it over and edge away to the bar as quickly as they decently can.

Because the stigma of the grieving person is that he or she is damaged, dark, tragic, and a downer to be around, you may find yourself fighting against being stigmatized. No one likes to be devalued into a set of cliché characteristics, so you may try extra hard to show the world you are not "that" by always displaying a mask of pleasant bravery.

But if you are grieving you will also discover the downside of doing this: that awful, sinking moment you experience after you are away from the people for whom you've been "pleasantly brave." When you get into your car alone, or shut the door behind them as they leave your house, you are free to remove the mask you wore for the comfort of others, and to sink like a stone. Not only are you as grief-stricken as ever, but you are that much more alienated from the rest of the world because of the show you have just put on.

If you are in grief, try not to worry about sparing others the truth of your situation. Don't suffer over *their* suffering. So what if they have to endure two minutes of fumbling awkwardness? What is it compared to what you must carry around? Try reaching out, even if it's in the same halting way that Bernie Williams went about it. Say: "I know you don't know what to say, so just hug me, or come sit and have a cup of coffee, or let's take a walk." You'll find that this kind of frank acknowledgment of the awkwardness of the situation usually eases it.

Of course, some people are thick. They deserve the dunce cap for emotional intelligence. And it can be surprising who will disappoint: the celebrated shrink, the churchgoer, your favorite bar-hopping friend may all fall short. But you will also find unsung emotional whizzes—the shrink's receptionist, a neighbor you didn't know well, someone old, someone young. Their intuitive grace around someone in grief will offset the many others who succumb to the stigma of it.

Of course, there are those who take a more "If you can't beat 'em, join 'em" approach to the way people stigmatize grievers. We overheard a lady in a crowded supermarket sat to a customer at the front of the checkout line, "Excuse me, sir, but my husband just died a few weeks ago. Can I cut in front of you?" Naturally the guy obliged. How could he not for (cue the sad, incidental music) a *widow*?

Good for her.

STUFF

The particulars of a life that are most concrete, most tangible and touchable, are one's possessions. Our things are a big part of who we are as people. I got "stuff," therefore I am. Comedian George Carlin did a famous routine about what he called "stuff" and its absurd overimportance in our lives.

> What is a house? It's just a pile of stuff with a cover. A house is a place to keep your stuff—while you go out and get more stuff! Ever noticed how the other guy's stuff is shit? But your shit is "stuff"!

When people die, they leave behind a lot of stuff, and because we view "things" as an extension of the person we lost, his or her possessions suddenly matter more than ever before. The person is gone, but we still have their stuff. In her book *A Very Easy Death*, Simone de Beauvoir writes about the last days of her mother:

> Everyone knows the power of things: life is solidified in them more immediately present than in any one of its instants. They lay there on the table, orphaned, useless, waiting to turn into rubbish or to find another identity.

De Beauvoir's insight came after seeing her sister react quite strongly to something belonging to their recently deceased mother. It was only a simple black hair ribbon, but the sister was overcome with feeling about it.

People told us how the most inconsequential everyday objects of a loved one who has died caused very strong emotion. One particular object that, for some reason, people have a powerful reaction to is shoes. In her memoir Joan Didion talks for pages about the struggle she had giving away her husband's shoes. At one point, after her book was published, an interviewer asked Didion how it was finally to give the shoes away.

She still hadn't.

The interview occurred five years after her husband's death, yet she continued to hold on to his shoes. We found it to be true in the people we talked to as well. In person after person, there's something about the shoes. Perhaps it's because shoes are the one article of clothing we don't wash or dry clean. The outline of a foot is worn into them, and the accumulated essence of the person is still there. In writing about the passing of his wife, the poet Donald Hall recalls, "He wept when the dog brought him a slipper that smelled of her still."

Sense of smell, as we know, is significantly linked to memory and can therefore provoke strong emotions. A waft of your loved one's scent on clothes may affect you like nothing else. As the writer Vladimir Nabokov observed, "Nothing revives the past so completely as a smell that was associated with it."

In the film *Brokeback Mountain*, one of the lovers, Ennis (played by Heath Ledger), visits the home of the other, Jack (played by Jake Gyllenhall). Jack has recently died, unexpectedly, without the two having had a chance for any kind of good-bye. When Ennis walks into Jack's room, the first thing he sees is his dead lover's denim jacket. He touches it, holds it up to his face, and inhales deeply. The audio fades up at this moment, so the audience hears Ledger inhaling. The filmmaker, Ang Lee, makes sure it is clear that when someone has gone, the act of smelling something matters. (After a second viewing, we noticed that, for a brief moment, before Ennis takes down the jacket he runs his hands over Jack's boots as well.)

A mother whose teenage son had died of a drug overdose told us another story. The boy was missing for a day and a half. While friends and family frantically searched for him, the mother had to busy herself so as not to go out of her mind with worry. She washed every article of her son's clothing because, in her words, "That's what moms do, right? We wash our guys' clothes." When the boy was found dead the next day, she was crestfallen to have no trace of him on the clothes she had washed.

Scent matters. All sorts of simple, taken-for-granted "stuff" matters.

Eyeglasses, too, carry a lot of power. Glasses seem not to be as great an issue if the person who died had an assortment of drugstore reading glasses around the house, as some people do. But if a loved one's glasses were a part of that person's face, they can cause devastatingly bittersweet feelings.

Then, of course, there are any number of miscellaneous trinkets that can blindside with sadness. The movie *In the Bedroom* is about a couple dealing with grief after the murder of their twenty-two-year-old son. After the boy's funeral, the father (played by Tom Wilkinson) walks into his son's room for the first time to look around and be there among his dead son's things. It's a scene that countless parents who have lost a child have lived through.

The father finds a small box filled with random keepsakes and looks through it. Suddenly he comes to something that stops him cold. A small piece of blue glass like you'd find on a beach, worn smooth by the tide. The father picks it up, and like a thunderclap the sobs come, tears flow and flow. There is no dialogue in the scene. Just feeling. What's the story behind the glass? Something they found together on vacation when his son was five? Who knows, and the film doesn't say. We never find out. Nor do we need to. We get the point.

Personal possessions become important, even sacred, after their owner has passed. If you find yourself on your knees by a dresser sniffing a sock, know that you are not crazy. Nor are you crazy if you have no desire to sniff anything, ever. People's reactions to "stuff" will differ, and with so many viewpoints to consider, deciding what to do with a loved one's belongings can be a fine line to walk.

A spouse certainly has the right to do what he or she wants with what is in the bedroom closet. But bear in mind that it could be tough for a son to come home the day after they bury mom and find a team of movers picking through her clothes, boxing them up, and hauling them away. The writer Philip Roth experienced this very thing when he arrived at his family's home after his mother's funeral. Mourners were filing in for the reception when Roth's Aunt Millie "rushed out of the bedroom . . . calling for help. 'You better go in there and do something, darling,' she whispered . . . 'your father's throwing everything out.'"

If you're talking about the belongings of a loved one who has died, phrases like "Give it away," "Throw it away," "Sell it," "Give it to the poor," "Let whoever wants it take it," make it sound like you're scattering them to the winds. But the objects of a life must eventually be relinquished.

Still, some people simply cannot or will not part with a loved one's things. They hold on to them in a way that stops being about a loved one's stuff and becomes about a need to hold on to it. The belongings of the dead can easily get mixed up with the emotional baggage of the living.

But most people do the best they can with the difficult task, trying hard to treat items with maximum dignity. Suse and Peter Lowenstein spoke at length about the gratitude they will forever feel for the way the citizens of Lockerbie, Scotland, cared for the passengers' personal items that were recovered from the wreckage of the plane crash that killed their son.

Flight 103 blew up in the air, 31,000 feet over Scotland, and the resulting debris was scattered over a field several miles wide. Everything that could be gathered by the police and recovery crews was stored. Given the circumstances of the crash, authorities thought there was too much of a potential chemical or bio hazard to do anything but dispose of it all. Understandably, the victims' families vehemently objected, and the local people of Lockerbie stepped up to help.

A group of women from the small town volunteered to handle the personal items, clean them, catalog them, and work with authorities and families to identify, as best they could, to what passengers they belonged. To this awful work they added the human touch that communities are sometimes capable of. They wrapped each item in fine tissue paper and twine, marked it with a dignified label, and sent these precious parcels to the families along with notes from the women of Lockerbie who had taken such good care of their loved one's "stuff."

A grace note indeed.

If the task of "doing something" falls upon you or someone close to you, there are common emotional sinkholes to be aware of.

Strangers, for example, will not have the emotional investment in the belongings of a loved one that you do—even though you will want them to. When you bring professionals into the situation you must be prepared for the ground rules of commerce. It's not easy to have some dealer in secondhand goods stand in your mother's living room and announce, "I'll give you seven hundred bucks for all of it." You'll want to throttle Maurice, the proprietor of Vintage Treasures or some such store, when he offers you ten dollars for the dress your mother wore on her honeymoon. But what can you expect? That Maurice will say, "Honeymoon? Oh, in that case I'll give you a thousand for it!" And would *that* be enough for you? Or any amount?

You must realize that these are not value judgments, merely the nature of sales. What price at the pawn shop could anyone hope to get for any of the cherished items we have mentioned— the blue glass in *In the Bedroom*, the denim jacket from *Brokeback Mountain*, the small ribbon that was Simone de Beauvoir's mother's, eyeglasses, a pair of slippers? Be careful not to expect the outside world to adhere to your value of such things.

Some people may also be greatly affected by the sense that an entire life is so easily contained in cardboard boxes and Hefty bags. It's hard to accept that someone you love can be reduced to a trunk or a truckload of odds and ends. You may ask yourself, "This is it? Is that all he was?"

There is no remedy for this, no suggestion that can alleviate the weight of this particular feeling. There's only the knowledge that everyone goes through it—"I read to know that I am not alone"—and that even the greatest lives may become a few finite items.

After John Lennon was murdered in December 1980, his wife, Yoko Ono, spoke of this feeling:

In early 1981, the Coroner's Office gave me back John's belongings in a plain brown paper bag. John was the King of the World. . . . John who had everything he could have wanted . . . came back to me in a brown paper bag in the end. I want the world to know that. I also want to show how many people have gone through similar tragedies.

Lennon may have left the world his music, but in the end, as a human, as John, he left his widow with old pens, razors, cigarette lighters, essentially whatever was lying around the house, and a paper bag of bloodstained clothes. They could have been anyone's.

Giving away someone's stuff is not so much about the goods themselves as it is about the giving away. If lives are made of little pieces that add up to a larger whole, possessions are a large part of the final sum. People are picky about what they choose to call "theirs." Someone always uses a specific coffee mug, or has a favorite baseball cap or a unique keychain. These things remain in the mind, forever associated with the person, especially after death. When garbage bags and boxes begin leaving the house filled with such items, it may be the first actualizing of those bits and pieces of them being wrenched away.

Parting with even the most random bits of a loved one's stuff is not easy. You'll be throwing out an old can of dried up shaving cream and think, "This was his," and suddenly find yourself holding an unofficial funeral for it: "Farewell, O can of Gillette Foamy. . . ." But the fact is letting go of small things feels like letting go of the person again.

While you know you can't keep a frozen flea-market of every single doodad someone owned, letting go of *anything* that once comprised a loved one's stuff can be difficult. But it has to happen.

ANVILS

Anvils were once used by blacksmiths for forging steel. The only place you might see one nowadays is in a rerun of an old cartoon where it's a common sight gag to drop one from a great height onto some unsuspecting character like Wile E. Coyote, flattening his head into a comic trapezoid from which two eyes peer out as if to say, "What just happened?"

Grieving people have anvils land on them all the time. It happens when, several months after a loss—and when one appears to be "doing okay"—he or she is clobbered by an emotion caused by an unexpected trigger. We use the word "anvil" to describe this aspect of grief—not in spite of its cartoon imagery but because of it. The way these moments arrive out of the clear blue sky, the ridiculous shape they may leave you in, and your hubris at having thought you were "holding up pretty well" are what make them anvils. They can make you feel like a fool, a rube, a cartoon.

You can never be sure what will make an anvil drop. They may have nothing at all to do with the circumstances of a loved one's death. This is the writer Colette's delicate description:

> It's so curious: one can resist tears and "behave" very
> well in the hardest hours of grief. But then someone
> makes you a friendly sign behind a window, or one
> notices that a flower that was in bud only yesterday has
> suddenly blossomed, or a letter slips from a drawer . . .
> and everything collapses.

Some anvils are related to a tragedy, but only in the most roundabout route through one's unconscious mind and sensory apparatus. There is the instance of a man who, as a young boy, had been in one of the lifeboats as the *Titanic* went down. As an old man he lived in Chicago, within earshot of Wrigley Field. He would grow distressed by the sound of the crowd whenever there was a home run. He said the distant roar sounded exactly like the doomed passengers wailing in the frigid water. Baseball is about as unrelated to the *Titanic* as you can get, but that's how anvils work.

Another woman was caring for her gravely ill brother. One day, against the doctors' orders, one of the brother's friends smuggled in vanilla ice cream and Fanta orange soda. The sick brother was thrilled to enjoy his favorites one more time before what they all knew was coming. Weeks later, after he died, the sister was getting lunch at work. She went to get a drink at the soda dispenser and there it was, a Fanta logo on one of the nozzles. BAM!

A flower, a home run, an orange soda—how do you guard against these things? You can't, which is what makes anvils so frustrating.

Entertainment anvils are common too: movies, TV, and radio can be loaded with them. There should be a movie rating for the bereft: RG—Restricted for Grievers, *Warning: May contain subject matter not suitable for an emotional basket case.* The good thing is, movie theaters are dark and people are always making noise in them anyway, so if you have to experience an anvil attack they're not a bad place for it. But find out a little about a movie beforehand. You don't want to go to see something like *Marley and Me* thinking it's a fun story about a dog and end up having the people in the row behind you saying, "Somebody help her."

Television can offer a potential blitz of anvils. Most grieving people get to be a pretty fast draw with the remote, ready to change the channel when they sense "Incoming!" Not only are there episodic programs with subject matter that may hit too close to home, there are also tearjerker commercials, heart-wrenching news stories, and upsetting talk-show topics to avoid. Even the pleasant shows can be a problem. TV people always look so damn happy, and since you're so damn *not*, they may hit you the wrong way.

Then there's the radio. Nothing in life ramps up emotion like music. At least with an iPod, after a loved one dies you can take certain songs off it and put them in a file marked "Someday maybe, not now." But listening to the radio, which most people do only while driving, is asking for trouble, and very few insurance companies will find sobbing to a Neil Young song an acceptable excuse for rear-ending another car.

Sometimes anvils are backdated. You'll get one from 1991, 1972, 1940. This happens when a distant but specific memory of the loved one takes you back to a younger time in your life. You'll be in a sporting goods store buying golf balls a few weeks after your father died when, all of a sudden, you're seventy-five pounds lighter, in Cub Scouts, trying to maneuver a canoe with him. Maybe you're a year out of college and your best friend dies. The next thing you know, you're backstage doing each other's makeup on opening night of the junior high musical.

These childhood memories may resurface as anvils during grief, but for some, especially people who lose parents, the anvil that comes is an actual childlike *feeling* and all the uncertainty that comes with it. As Ralph Waldo Emerson said, "Sorrow makes us all children again."

The writer Christopher Buckley, son of William F. Buckley, Jr., chronicled the loss of both his parents within an eleven-month period in his book *Losing Mum and Pup: A Memoir.* Buckley refers to the experience as "an account of becoming an orphan." He admits that "'orphan' sounds like an overdramatic term for becoming parentless at age fifty-five," but Buckley came to find he was not alone in his feelings of fresh "orphanhood," even in middle age.

I was struck by the number of times the word ["orphan"] occurred in the 800 or more condolence letters I received

after my father died. . . . "Now you're an orphan" . . . "I
know the pain myself of being an orphan" . . . "You must
feel so lonely, being an orphan" . . . "When I became an
orphan it felt like the earth dropping out from under me."

The anvils that hit Buckley, along with many others, are anvils
of feeling unprotected, unsupervised, a little like being sent
down the river in a basket.

Even if you experience none of these anvils that "take you
back," there will surely be others that make you highly aware
of the present. The poet and painter Dante Gabriel Rossetti
wrote, "Beauty without the beloved is like a sword through the
heart." As life moves forward, there will be plenty of beautiful moments from which your beloved will be absent. Even the
most wonderful moments of life will now be targets for anvils.
No matter how sunny the day, how perfect the meal, how tem-
perate the water, there will always be part of you that knows
the departed is not there enjoying it with you. It may feel like a
"sword through the heart."

Initially you may be overwhelmed by the terrible thing
that's happened, but grief isn't only about a bad thing that happened. It's also about all the good things that won't happen. You
will begin to realize all the occasions your loved one won't be
around for: the birth of a child, a graduation, or—one we heard
a lot—a wedding. Young girls we spoke with who lost a father
all brought up "walking down the aisle" without him.

An anvil may be expected, but it can still be heavy and fall
hard. On holidays, for example, you know they're coming, but
they're still tough. No longer occasions for carefree fun, holidays become, for at least the first few years, something "to get
through." The trimmings and trappings of Christmas and their
ubiquity in our culture can make December feel like it's snowing

anvils. Those unavoidable carols with their lyrics of warm fires, frosty nights, olden days, and gingerbread, all sung to bittersweet melodies. Is it any wonder people get blotto on eggnog?

In dealing with holidays, making a few small changes to family rituals can help. One family always ate Christmas dinner, rather formally, around their large dining room table. The family had several siblings, all in their thirties and forties, so with the addition of spouses and children and grandchildren the table eventually needed two big leaves and a card-table caboose for the kids. Each year the meal would begin with the patriarch saying grace.

But the year one of the beloved siblings died, the family matriarch had the idea that everyone should eat buffet style, plates on laps, in the big TV room with a ball game on. When the family gathered around, filling their plates at the island in the kitchen, everyone was aware of the person who was not there. But it wasn't as glaring and awkward as it would have been had they all been at the dining room table in "missing man formation." They might as well have had an anvil for a centerpiece.

If you always eat out on Christmas, stay in. If you always go to one kind of restaurant, go to another. Grandma may protest: "Benihana's for Christmas dinner? Over my dead body." Tell her the grandchildren will love it.

Everyone knows that the "first holidays" after a loved one dies are difficult, and there's a big sigh of relief come January. But the second year can be even harder. High-maintenance relatives who were on good behavior the first year probably won't be the second time around, and you may also have let down your guard too much, assuming the "sophomore" year will be easier. Sophomores, as anyone who has been to college knows, think they know it all. Watch out for year two.

Other anvils come at night. It's quiet, you're alone, and your mind is free to wander. You're a sitting duck. This is especially true on nights when you wake and can't get back to sleep. (It's not easy to sleep under an anvil.) Interestingly, three different people cited the exact same time to us as being the worst: "4:30 A.M."

It makes sense. By 4:30 you've slept enough not to be able to nod off again. But it's dark and too early to get up. The newspaper hasn't come, the morning talk shows aren't yet on, and no friends are awake to phone. (Some people lie there canvassing who they know in other time zones.) There's nothing to do but watch the changing numerals on your alarm clock. Tick, and after what seems like forever, tock.

Finally, the anvils that may be the most soul-changing have to do with other grieving people. Susan Sontag wrote in her book *Illness as Metaphor* that "Everyone who is born holds dual citizenship, in the kingdom of the well and in the kingdom of the sick." For at least a while, she says, we will all end up "identifying ourselves" as "citizens of that other place."

Grief has a similar citizenship.

Those who now find themselves in this "other place"—those who now live in the land where anvils fall—can recognize their fellow citizens. Joan Didion says:

> People who have recently lost someone have a certain look, recognizable maybe to those who have seen that look on their own faces. I have noticed it on my face and I notice it on others.

She describes "that look" as similar to someone leaving the eye doctor's office after having their pupils dilated, or someone who has to wear glasses walking around without them. C. S. Lewis knew the look and gave it a word: concussed. Suse Lowenstein says she recognizes the look in the way some grieving people hold their bodies. In fact she began *Dark Elegy* when she noticed how another mother who had lost someone on PanAm Flight 103 moved and carried herself. Suse asked if she could sculpt her.

This look is not something just anyone can spot. The people Didion talks about don't act like Mr. Magoo; the people Suse notices don't move like zombies. It's subtler, something you become sensitive to only after having been through it yourself. Grieving people are highly sensitized to other grieving people, even if they don't wish to be. Emily Dickinson wrote:

> I measure every grief I meet
> With analytic eyes;
> I wonder if it weighs like mine,
> Or has an easier size.

To see other people in grief can be a difficult and unexpected reminder of everything you've been through. Grieving people gain an empathy that nongrieving people may lack. It can be painful, but it restores an instinct that our modern world has a way of diminishing.

We are a culture of overstimulation and undermined ethics. Madison Avenue figured out long ago that the selfish are much more apt to buy things than the empathic. Is it any wonder that ad after ad treats narcissism as a virtue? Add to this the way technology has increased the time we spend in purely personal space and in a purely personal mind-set: personal computers, iPods, televisions, self-tailored websites. As George Harrison said, "All through the day: I, me, mine." Grief, for better or worse, opens a person up to the rest of the world, and for some people this is a great change.

One woman had a boss who was a first-class monster, one of those men who loves making his subordinates miserable, and for whom the woman could do no right. When her mother died of old age at ninety-two, the boss got wind of it and suddenly turned into a pussycat. It turned out his grandmother had died a few years before in her nineties, and he was appalled at how little people seemed to care about the death of someone that age and the wrenching effects it can have on a person. The boss had clearly suffered a few anvils of his own. He talked heart-to-heart with the woman, actually gave her a bit of extra time off, and one day even hugged her. Of course within a week or so he was back to being a monster, but the empathy was nice while it lasted.

If you are already a fairly empathic person, learning about grief will fine-tune that empathy. If you are not a particularly empathic person, grief can be the eye-opener of a lifetime. In all of Shakespeare there is no more purely pigheaded character than King Lear. He starts off with everything and ends up as we previously described him: in rags, holding his dead daughter, and babbling the word "Never."

During that steep decline in his fate, Lear has some pauses and, it could be argued, some epiphanies. Having been stripped of his throne, his kingdom, and even his shelter, Lear begins to think about all the poor and homeless people who, wherever they are, are out in the cold rain like him. His suffering opens him up to the suffering of others in a way that has not happened before, a revelation so strong that Lear's words become almost prayerlike.

> Poor naked wretches, wheresoe'er you are
> That bide the pelting of this pitiless storm,
> How shall your houseless heads and unfed sides,
> Your looped and windowed raggedness, defend you
> From seasons such as these? O, I have taken

Too little care of this! Take physic, pomp;
Expose thyself to feel what wretches feel,
That thou mayest shake the superflux to them
And show the heavens more just.

Of course the heavens don't feel very "just" when you are in grief, not when you're going through life trying to dodge falling anvils. It helps to know that other people are going through the same thing and that you are not alone. But it doesn't make the weight of all those "nevers" any lighter.

CHAPTER TWO

PROCESSING HONESTLY

THE WORK

"Grief is a beginning."

Although this is the kind of phrase one reads in chirpy self-help books that make grief tidier than it is, we begin this chapter with these words because they are, indeed, true. Grief *is* a beginning. But it's not a beginning in the cheery "It's a new day!" connotation of the word. Grieving is not like gazing at a mountain sunrise from a white porch on a balmy morning, like a commercial for one of those cereals that's good for you. Grief is a beginning all right, but a beginning of hard, messy work.

The hardest and messiest job of all is being honest with yourself, honest about everything: you, the person you have lost, what happened in your past, what will not happen in your future. Grief is such an onslaught of raw truth that few people emerge from it without their relationship to truth itself altered. Grief makes some people more honest, some people less so.

The people who seem to come through grief with what you might call their "life force" still intact are those who have been most honest.

This was a lesson we received in the very first seconds of meeting Suse and Peter Lowenstein. They live on the waterfront in Montauk, Long Island. On our initial visit we drove up to what, according to the house number on the large stone gate-post, was their place. But, oddly, the name on the gate was not Lowenstein. The sign said: Tundergarth.

We drove onto the property anyway and realized that we had the right place when Suse, all smiles, came out to greet us. After a minute of small talk we asked, "Why does the gate out front say, Tundergarth?" Suse answered:

> Oh, Tundergarth is the name of the farm in Lockerbie
> where Alexander's body was found. We got to know the
> couple who own the place. They're wonderful. The word
> "tundergarth" means "away from the wind." That's a nice
> phrase, isn't it? Well, come on in, we'll have some coffee.

This was our first experience with the frankness we came to know as the standard way Suse and Peter talk about Alex, his fate, and their lives without him.

But it quickly became apparent that this frankness about what happened to their son sits side by side with another quality that anyone who spends time with the Lowensteins can see: they have a remarkable capacity for joy and, as we came to find out, are damn fun people to know. Peter is a retired business-man who now spends much of his time flying the two of them all over the East Coast in his small plane. Suse is a professional artist who sculpts in a large studio adjacent to their house. Both are avid scuba divers. They are parents (of Lucas, Alexander's younger brother) and exuberant grandparents to his three kids.

To meet the Lowensteins is to realize that two incongru-ous things are true about them. On the one hand, the worst thing that could befall parents happened to them: they lost a child, through violence, to terrorism. On the other hand, they embrace life fully. The words *carpe diem*, "seize the day," were on the screensaver on the computer in Suse's studio.

The Lowensteins' ability to take all aspects of life, the joyful and the celebratory alongside the wicked and the unjust, and fully incorporate them into their life is at the center of the honesty we are talking about. It's a willingness to accept all facets of the truth. As Joan Didion said in an interview, when it comes to grief, "You have to look in the eye whatever is likely to undo you."

But many grieving people cannot. They can't bring themselves to "look in the eye" what is likely to undo them. The "bad things" are not considered or mentioned. While you may choose this as one way to go, something may happen to you regarding the "good things" too. In order to keep "bad truth" out, you may develop a kind of "truth filter"—an internal mechanism to stop upsetting things from penetrating you too deeply. While the mechanism can work to keep the demons at bay, it tends to remain in place all the time, demons or not. As a result, the truth filter also keeps out "good truths" as well. Your pain of losing someone is forbidden, but so too may be the full joy of who you are and what you have.

Many long-term grievers give you the sense that they are not so much feeling great pain but rather are unable to feel great joy—the downside of that self-protective truth filter. Because the Lowensteins have no truth filter to keep out the bad truth of what happened to their son, they are also fully open to all truths. This includes the good truths, the truths that bring them happiness today—the ocean, grandchildren, travel, their life together.

Resisting this truth filter is a big part of the work of grief. As far as we can tell, the only way to do it is with words.

There's no getting around it. Things must be said in some form—even if it's only to oneself. Shakespeare, who himself knew grief so well, expressed this belief in no uncertain terms:

Give sorrow words. The grief that does not speak Whispers o'er the fraught heart and bids it break.

Grief will speak one way or another, either by means of your putting it into words, or by inner whispers to the heart that never let you heal. Honest words are a remedy. As Aeschylus said, "Words are the physician of the diseased mind." Beyond grief, the chief means by which people are restored to emotional health often involve speaking honest words: from twelve-step recovery programs in which people go to meetings for years saying over and over, "Hi. My name is Mary, and I'm an alcoholic," to the religious practice of confession, to psychoanalysis (which Germaine Greer calls "confession without absolution"). Emotional healing requires words.

Knowing that words can be a "physician of the mind" is of great help particularly to a grieving person. If you've been through an experience of illness or the death of a loved one, you've been in situations where the hard things were not put into words. There is a poem that Billy Collins wrote about his father's inability to let himself hear the word "cancer." Instead, the ill man keeps pretending that his son is saying "campfire." True, cancer is one of the big no-no words, and lots of people try to avoid it. But not talking about something doesn't mean it hasn't done its damage. And you can't bring a loved one back to life by using the "campfire" way of talking about how they died. What can be preserved is your relationship with the truth, but it only happens by giving voice to honest words.

Many grieving people accomplish this through psychiatry or support groups. The value of psychiatry is that, because you pay someone to hear you put your feelings into words, you don't have to feel that you're a burden. You also pay for confidentiality, which is no small thing if you don't like the idea of a deep conversation becoming a dinner-table anecdote.

The value of support groups is that they are organized. Volatile and awkwardly personal talk is protected by the support group's regimented meeting times and mannerly ways of doing things. Discussion is promoted, people take turns, conversational lulls are handled—all of which can constitute helpful training wheels if you are a hesitant communicator.

But however helpful these two approaches may be, many people find them appalling. Some people consider that any kind of psychiatry has a stigma to it. They equate it with being crazy rather than with grieving. Saying to such a person, "Why don't you see someone?" is like saying, "Why don't you walk around wearing a straitjacket?"

For some people, the same is true about support groups. The idea of crying on a stranger's shoulder may terrify you. (Interestingly, sometimes the person who is most afraid of a support group ends up benefiting most from it.)

If neither of these avenues appeals to you, fine. It doesn't mean that you can't achieve honesty just because you're skittish about sharing feelings with others. Being truthful doesn't mean you have to make a public confession of intimate feelings. "Honesty" doesn't mean that you start a blog called *Peeling the Onion of My Woe*. Honesty is merely a commitment to try to be truthful, especially to *yourself*. If you don't feel like sharing with others, put grief into words for yourself alone.

Many people find that writing helps. David Grossman, who has written extensively about his son Uri who was killed in the 2006 Israeli-Lebanon conflict, regards "the correct and precise use of words" as "a remedy to illness" (note the word-as-physician idea again) and "a contraption for purifying the air." Some people find there is great power in making it "actual" by imprinting their feelings in words with ink on paper.

Try it. Pick up a notebook, or turn on the computer and begin jotting. You don't have to show your writing to anyone, you don't even have to keep it. We talked with people about a trick that works pretty well. Go to a café, preferably one you never frequent, and sit there writing the most painfully honest words. When you're done, tear up the pages and throw them in the garbage. And that's that. You will have done what's necessary, you will have put things into words.

This is pretty much what Joan Didion and C. S. Lewis did. Yes, both were accomplished writers before they wrote books on grief, but neither intended to write on the subject. Initially they sat down to write as a way of sorting through the swarm of feelings and thoughts they were experiencing.

Didion clicked on her computer a week after her husband died and wrote four blunt sentences. It wasn't until writing what she called "notes" for some time that she realized she was beginning to structure a book. She told her publishers she was leery about the subject being so "purely personal," and later she admitted that her writing had never been so "raw," so intimately honest.

The same thing happened with C. S. Lewis. Being a professor at Oxford, like most teachers he had many half-empty notebooks lying around the house. He began jotting in one of them, and four notebooks later he had written a classic. Lewis was actually so fearful about putting such intimate feelings into such nakedly honest words that his book was first published under a pen name, N. W. Clerk, something he had never done.

If writing doesn't suit you, you can always just say the words out loud. Alone. You may feel more comfortable being like the character in Shakespeare who says, "I tell my sorrows to the stones." It's still honesty.

So say it. Say it with no one else around. Say it in the empty backyard or to the shower curtain. Shout it in the car alone or walking in the woods. This is the work of grief.

PANIC

Grief comes without warning, often in an instant, and when it does it changes everything. The instant almost always takes you by surprise. People usually say, "I *never* thought it would happen to me." They don't say, "I only *occasionally* thought it would happen to me." Even when a death is expected, as when a loved one is ill and the end is sure, it's surprising how many people say they were nonetheless taken by surprise when death finally came.

All grief begins with the awful instant.

The whole notion of this "instant" is so harrowing and intimate that grieving people rarely talk about it. Grief books talk about the days, weeks, months, and years after a death, but few, if any, deal with the very minutes, or even seconds, after losing a loved one.

Even a book as frank as Didion's leaves out the "instant." She describes everything leading up to and including her husband's heart attack. She describes everything that happens when the paramedics arrive to try to save him. And she thoroughly describes her year-long subsequent grief. But she omits the "instant." The moments between the heart attack and the arrival of the paramedics are left unaccounted for. It could only have been a few minutes, time Didion most likely spent lost in panic, but they are significant because it's *panic* that makes the "instant" so horrible.

If you are in grief, chances are you feel a kind of low-grade panic much of the time. Underneath, grief can be the suspenseful feeling that something bad may happen again at any second. You fear that God may be getting ready to drop the other shoe.

Many grieving people live with this feeling. The very first line of C. S. Lewis's book is: "No one ever told me that grief felt so like fear." This feeling is not a fear of something specific so much as it's a generalized presence of fear hovering over all of your life. "I am not afraid," Lewis explains, "but the sensation is like being afraid. The same fluttering in the stomach, the same restlessness."

If you recognize this feeling in the stomach, this vague, wrenching restlessness in your gut, it will help you to understand the dynamics of panic as they relate to grief. But the truth is that panic is unsettling even to think about or discuss. Just the topic of panic may make you panic! People can grieve with dignity, but you don't hear about people panicking with dignity. Panic is nightmarish; it makes us utter sounds and contort our faces and bodies in ways we never have before; it makes us lose control and become different than we usually are. All of this is chilling to experience or witness.

But we've included the subject of panic in this chapter on honesty because it's important to understand that panic is also a kind of dishonesty. Panic is a lie.

Panic is part of our evolutionary wiring, a primal sensation no doubt meant to warn our cavemen-selves of impending trouble. But we are no longer cavemen, and moreover in grief the trouble isn't impending, it's already happened. The loved one has died; there's nothing anyone can do about that. So what good is panic? None. That chilling flood of adrenaline released by our panic mechanism is not only a dreadful sensation, it's also a false alarm, as counterfeit as ringing the firebell after a house has already burned to the ground.

Because panic is such a primal mechanism that can overtake a human being so completely, for those present at a scene of panic, the anguish it causes is more intense than the worst sadness. Which situation, for example, would be worse to witness: seeing a person at the funeral of a loved one, or seeing that same person being told the loved one had been killed? Is there anyone who wouldn't think the second situation far worse? Why so unanimous a reaction given that in both cases the loved one is dead and the survivor devastated? The reason is that the second case would produce a scene of panic, which for most people is hard to bear.

Of course, you don't usually get to decide whether you are present at a scene of panic. The moment is thrust upon you. Every day there are people put in the situation of having to give tragic news to a family member, an acquaintance, or even a co-worker whom they may not even know well. It's common that, when a tragedy happens, a person is summoned from the normal workday routine to be told the news by a boss, a colleague, a secretary.

Dr. Yves Duroseau of St. Vincent's Hospital in Manhattan wrote of an occasion in which he had to inform the family of a woman in his care that she had unexpectedly died. He was compelled to write the article, he said, because of how woefully ill-equipped even accomplished professionals are when it comes to dealing with panic. He felt "a sense of helplessness and a sense of not being equipped or trained to deal with these things." If a doctor can feel so unprepared for the situation, how much more so will be the teacher telling a child, the boss telling an employee, the husband telling his wife, or the grieving person who keeps turning over phantom panics in his or her nervous mind?

Dr. Duroseau's situation did not go well at all. As he describes it, it began as a professional nightmare for him and quickly escalated into chaos.

As soon as I said, "Your mother has passed away," the screaming, yelling, and crying started. People were on the floor. People were running up and down the hallway. People were grabbing me, crying—"How did this happen, how could this happen? Are you sure she died? Is this a mistake? Is it somebody else?"

Just imagining this scene is enough to make someone head for the hills, anything to escape the terrifying panic. But examining the methodology of this monster can help demystify it.

The word "panic" comes from Pan, a god in Greek mythology. Most people assume that since the emotion of panic is his namesake, Pan must have been a god who jumped around nervously. (He is depicted as half man and half goat—plenty of reason to be jumpy.) But it was another aspect of this god that gave birth to the word "panic." Pan was a god of the woodlands who was responsible for the frightening noises travelers heard when they were in the woods alone. He caused something called *panikon deima*, or sudden fear in lonely places.

This primal human emotion is expressed in mythological terms as being, first, about feeling alone and unprotected, and second, about being scared of strange sights and sounds, unfamiliar stimuli akin to a ghoulish goat-god rustling the reeds. Taking this point of view, your panic may be diminished if you realize you are *not* alone, and if there is a minimum of frenzied stimuli coming at you. To know this, either intuitively or by acquiring an understanding of it, can go a long way toward disarming panic in even the worst situations.

In Dr. Duroseau's case, he admits that his medical training was of little help in the face of a grieving family's panic. Instead he was forced to fall back on his innate humanity—the emotional equivalent of Luke Skywalker shutting off the techno-gadgets and using "The Force." Duroseau writes:

> I realized very quickly that there were no words of comfort that would help make them feel better, that nothing that I said could really help. At that point, I had to shift gears. The family needed time and space to get their emotions out, but we couldn't have people running up and down the hallways. I was trying to respect their needs but at the same

time protect the other patients' space. I got help almost immediately, because everyone was aware that we needed to contain the situation. Security came to help, nurses and social workers to speak with the family.

The family was made to feel safe and protected, and the situation became controlled and somewhat less hysterical than it had been only moments earlier.

So few things can be done in a time of crisis to make things better. You can't turn back the clock and make someone who has just died live again. You can't protect yourself from a future life without the loved one who has died. And Dr. Duroseau was right in concluding there is nothing to be said that will make the bereaved feel better. But try not to make things worse by flooding the situation with the chaotic energy of panic that helps nothing. It's like a car accident where the horn gets stuck. Bad enough there's been an accident, but can't someone at least disengage that goddam screeching horn?!

Notice that the first thing Dr. Duroseau did when he realized he was in over his head was to get help from other people. The people who are on hand to help at a time of crisis matter a great deal. If you have any say as to who is there to help, choose people judiciously and sparingly. Involving too many people will make your situation more difficult. When you are in panic you will look for someone to connect with; feeling pulled between an array of people can make you feel *more* alone, which in turn will make you feel more panicky.

Remember too that people can become different in a panicked situation than they are in normal life. Dependable people can turn to jelly, and the person everyone thinks is high-strung often turns out to be strung with steel.

Some people are not helpful in a panicked situation. In particular, beware of "doers." They may be useful in a plumbing catastrophe but not when someone has just learned that a loved one has died. That's because there is nothing for them to "do," only something for them to "be." Unable to "be," they will look for something—anything!—to *do*. While doers mean well and want to help, much of what they do can make things worse. In the movie *The Producers*, when Gene Wilder freaks out and keeps repeating, "I'm hysterical! I'm hysterical!" Zero Mostel throws a glass of water in his face. After a pause, Wilder says, "I'm wet! I'm wet! I'm still hysterical and I'm wet!" This is the kind of contribution "doers" can make. Get them away from the situation by saying something like, "Harry, you are the only person I can trust to pull the car around," even if you don't need the car pulled around.

For centuries, whenever a woman went into labor the old standby phrase that people shouted was "Boil some water!" Over the years people have come to realize that boiled water is not the slightest bit necessary to a birth. The point of asking for it was to give husbands something to do (husbands are notorious doers), something to occupy them in a way that did no harm.

Finally, there is the issue of information, the brute facts of the situation that create the awful instant. Something terrible has happened, and that information must be absorbed. The initial challenge in receiving this news is to take it in, understand what has happened, and realize that it is true. It is best to have that information in precise language. In a time of panic, it's easy to misinterpret what you hear. We heard a story in which a teacher at a school died. An administrator whose job it was to deliver the news said to another teacher, "Mr. Johnson had a fatal heart attack," to which the teacher responded, "Oh my God! Is he all right?"

Bearers of bad news often like to use fuzzy words or euphemisms rather than be direct. They say things like, "He's gone," or, "We lost him." In a heightened situation you might miscon-strue them. ("He's gone? You mean he's not in his room?" or, "We lost him? Well, let's find him.") You should say that a loved one has *died*. Use the word "dead." Not putting the truth into words won't make it go away, won't make it easier to accept.

At awful times it is difficult to be honest. Honesty won't alleviate the sadness and the tragedy that has occurred, but it does reduce the panic. Weathering the dreaded crucible of an "instant" takes terrible courage. Ernest Hemingway famously defined courage as "grace under pressure." But when it comes to grief, perhaps the poet Phillip Larkin's definition is more apt. To him, courage means "not scaring people."

SHAME

A man was telling us the story of his father who, a year before, had died at age eighty-five. The father had been a Chicago cop, married fifty-three years to the same woman, had six kids, sev-enteen grandkids, a devoted Catholic, great Irish sense of humor, loved by all.

But as the man talked about his father's later years it became apparent that something about his father troubled him. He acted like there was something shameful he was about to tell us. He began speaking more haltingly, heavily, like he was carrying a burden. What was the drama? A long-lost love child? A crime? Finally he told us the deep dark secret: "In the last two years of his life, my father was pissing himself."

All this pent-up shame over *that*? Our response caught the man by surprise: "So what. It's not that big a deal." But to the son it was a big deal. He said he was embarrassed seeing a strong, proud man like his father having to endure that.

Many people who have been in either role—older parent or caretaker son/daughter—can relate to this feeling. In a beautiful line in Marilynne Robinson's novel *Gilead*, the older, now diminished narrator says, "How I wish you could have known me in my strength." Many people in the position of the dying father seem to be crying out these words, or at least their loved ones can sense them.

Shame is one of the most unspoken aspects of grief. It was surprising to find what strong feelings of shame people have about issues related to grief and dying, issues not only beyond their control but completely natural and inevitable parts of being human.

This secret shame that grieving people carry is so widespread, so common, that it must be somehow ingrained in our culture. This is not so much a shortcoming of our way of life as it is a by-product of certain aspects of the American character that we love and others admire. Americans are about the future, about youth, health, and vigor, and about fun. (Is there any public event we can't turn into a tailgate party?) Above all, America is about winning—or at least not losing.

We are not a culture that accepts loss of any kind well, whether it's on the battlefield or the ball field, in the court of law or the court of public opinion. We can't even abide being outmaneuvered for the last free parking space on the block. Loss is an American taboo. The most common word we use as a catchall devaluation of someone is *loser*.

We are surrounded by advertisements telling us that even the most natural of human losses, things like hair, skin tone, cleavage, and sexual potency need not be accepted. (Some of the men in those Viagra ads look old enough to be pitchmen for Dentucreme.) This inability to accept loss of any kind has shaped the feelings of many individuals about themselves and others. It has made for some unhealthy, unsustainable notions about loss in general and, more specifically, about death and its aftermath of grief.

Death and grief are diametric opposites of those fine American qualities of "the future" and "youth" and "health" and "vigor" and "fun." Dying people and grieving people are losers. Cultural messages that say loss is unnatural make people who suffer loss feel like they are an aberrant exception, like something is wrong with them.

Read any day's obituary column and you'll see that people don't "suffer" or "die" from diseases, they "lose" their "courageous," "valiant" battles with cancer or other ailments. While the idea that death is something you "fight" against may help a sick person who needs to summon the energy to stay as healthy as possible, the downside of this win-lose mentality is that when death finally approaches, a specter of "failure" descends upon the scene.

A girl told us that one of the last things her father said to her before he died of a recurrence of lymphatic cancer was that he had really tried to beat the disease but just couldn't. He kept saying, "I'm so sorry, but I tried." This was a man who had been a beloved teacher, a loving husband, a father of three—and also an amateur clown at charitable events. But he died feeling like a failure because, well, *because* he was dying.

The idea that death is a failure or something to be ashamed of is rampant, even in the way we treat our dead. Most Americans are teenagers or older by the time they see a dead body, and when they do go to a typical American funeral they find a scene of intense cultural airbrushing. The vestibule of just about every funeral parlor looks like it was decorated by someone's tasteful maiden aunt, and everything in the "viewing room" is bathed in soft, pastel colors—from the lighting to the flowers to the dead person.

There is nothing natural about it. The message is loud and clear that death is unnatural. (The only time we say that someone has died of "natural causes" is when the person is so old we don't think he or she was having much of a life anyway.)

We aren't as good as other cultures at incorporating death as a part of life. When someone dies we act like something is *wrong*, when in fact nothing is. Life has run its unavoidable course. Other cultures, in which death is recognized fully as a part of life, do not have this same sense that a death is something wrong. Sad, yes. But not wrong.

A woman told us a story about being at a funeral for her relative. It was a typically staid event, family and friends standing around awkwardly, their arms down in front of them with one hand crossed over the other—the official American I'm-at-a-wake stance. In the viewing room next to theirs was a family of Filipino immigrants, there for the wake of the elderly family matriarch. The place was mobbed with people, talking as freely and loudly as if they were gathered around a kitchen table instead of a coffin. Kids of all ages were everywhere, hanging around the casket, even climbing up on it with the help of adults to have a look at their dead great-grandmother. And they were videotaping it, taking pictures of the deceased in her casket!

Run this scene by the average American mother and ask if she'll let her six-year-old go to a wake. Most of them will say, "Not a chance."

Of course, people can't easily overturn their cultural inclinations. Not many Americans will want a picture of dead grandma, laid out in lavender, as their screen-saver. But the by-product of this skittishness is that death is viewed as abnormal and therefore abhorrent. And so too are the sick, the dying, the dead, the grieving.

If you are grieving, you may carry images in your mind that you cannot shake—mental pictures of illness and death that sometimes play and replay in your mind in an endless, tormenting loop. Most of these images deal with the physical body and what it goes through in the process of shutting down. Sick people vomit, and worse. Hurt people bleed, and worse. Old men

piss themselves, and worse. What makes these images so difficult to deal with is *shame*.

Dr. Sherwin Nuland's book *How We Die* explains in clear language the anatomical details of how people die from a variety
of causes. This book may help you understand what your loved
one went through, help you see the body as physical machinery
rather than a vehicle of suffering or death. But for many people
the information is horrifying. Even people outside of grief may
have their skin crawl when confronted with "body stuff." Consider what one book reviewer wrote of Nuland's book:

> In its pages lungs fill up with water, oxygen is cut off,
> arteries collapse, livers enlarge, kidneys are poisoned,
> tumors grow, cancers spread, intestines do things you really
> don't want to know about. I read 50 or so of its gruesome
> pages before squeamishness prevented my finishing.

If a person whose job it is to read for a living can't even make
it through a book about how bodies shut down, where on earth
does that leave people like the man in Chicago who literally
must watch it happen?

It's not a complete surprise that people feel shame about illness. After all, most Americans carry a cultural sensitivity about
bodily imperfections throughout their lives, from acne to a
walker. But it is a surprise to see how many people feel shame
about losing a loved one.

After a loved one dies, you may feel that *you* did something
wrong by losing the person who is gone, however absurd that
may be. It's reminiscent of Lady Bracknell's snarky line from *The
Importance of Being Earnest*: "To lose one parent may be regarded
as a misfortune, to lose both looks like carelessness." Grieving
people often *do* feel this way, as if they have been careless, as if
they didn't hold on tightly enough, as if somehow they blew it.

Like sickness and death, people also treat the process of grieving as shameful. A failure. A failure to "get on with it," to "get back in the swing of things." People will say about a grieving person—and in fact grievers will say it about themselves—"It's been almost eight months and she's *still* not over it." But if you broke every bone in your body in an accident, no one would expect you to be back as the demon of the racquetball court in just a few months.

We have no patience for grief. We hope that people will finally just experience "closure," which is usually just code for "Hey, can we stop being depressed about your loss and start talking about *my* problems again?" That's why it was so nice to hear this pesky buzzword slammed by Katie Couric, who lost her husband to colon cancer at age forty-two. She called closure "the most hated word by every grief-stricken individual in the world."

All this shame, secretly attached to death and dying, can leave you feeling exiled on the island of taboo. And on the remotest part of that island are the kinds of images we began with—a man ashamed of his father's natural processes shutting down. These indignities will always be the worst pictures and evoke the greatest shame, because, in the words of Albert Camus, "It is not pain that must arouse pity but indignity."

Dying, as much as we would like to sanitize it, is a tough and ugly process. And a dead body, while no longer suffering, is not much prettier. Sherwin Nuland says it directly: "I have not often seen much dignity in the process by which we die." But he follows this with a comment that rescues the whole gruesome enterprise from despair.

> If there is wisdom to be found, it must be in the knowledge that human beings are capable of the kind of love and loyalty that transcends not only physical debasement but even the spiritual weariness.

Being able to weather indignity with grace is itself a version of dignity. And a reversal of shame.

If you carry around uncomfortable images of shaving, cleaning, wiping, holding, or dressing someone who was ill, or if you carry equally agonizing images of someone after death—so small, so diminished, so much more body than being—you can take a measure of pride in having done what Shakespeare says is a requirement of all great love, which is "to bear it out even to the edge of doom."

These experiences are not shames but medals of emotional valor. You have borne it out, gone the distance, kept poised amid ugly sights, and bucked up the faltering dignity of someone you loved. You may in time even come to cherish having done the hard things and witnessed those uncomfortable moments that turned into bad images. You may feel thankful for the opportunity to show the dying, and yourself, and the heavens the measure of your love. You may even feel lucky. Donald Hall, who cared for his dying wife through a dreadful illness, said of the experience, "Her death was the worst thing that could happen and caring for her the best."

The hope is to achieve a measure of absolution from this odd shame that is attached to grief, the shame of loss and indignity. A large part of grief involves getting to a place where you can, as odd as it may sound, *forgive*. Forgive human beings for having bodies that bleed and break and weep and shit and fail. And forgive yourself for having someone you love die and for feeling so lost without them.

TRUST

"Never throw them a rope that you don't have the other end of."

We came to think of this expression as one of the wisest comments we heard about how to communicate with someone in grief. Said offhandedly by a psychologist, it became a rule of thumb for us. The idea is simple: no matter how well intentioned it may be, one should not tell someone in grief anything that can't be backed up.

If, for example, a person says, "She's in a better place," it's a rope that the person cannot possibly be holding the other end of. No one can know for sure that the loved one is in a so-called better place. If someone says, "Don't worry, you'll be all right," again that person is throwing you a rope that can't be held. How can someone presume to say, "You'll be all right" when you yourself don't know that?

On the other hand, if someone says, "I can see how much you loved him," that's something the person can know with some assurance. That's a rope you can grab knowing that someone will be holding the other end. Even better if the person says, "I'll keep my cell phone on all night, and I promise if your number comes up I'll answer anytime." That's something the person can know, and do. That's a rope you can trust.

The solidity of "ropes" has a lot to do with language. Most of us go through life unconcerned with the conversational hyperboles and false niceties we habitually say to one another. What else can you say to the weird neighbor you bump into while getting the mail except "how nice the weather is," even if you don't really mean it? There's normally no need to call people on the benign dishonesty of language. We don't say, "What do you mean you'll be there for me 24/7? Aren't you ever going to sleep?"

When you are in grief, however, language matters more. This is because you may be skittish about trusting anything, even something said by the most well-meaning friend, loved one, or acquaintance.

Grief is largely a crisis of trust. When you lose a loved one you lose a major trust in the basic "okayness" of life. One moment life was fine, the next, something happened that rocked your world. For some, the moment is a long process—it began with the idle comment from your spouse who noticed something while in the shower. A year later it would end in his or her death. For others it's more sudden: life is fine one second, and the next it's in smithereens. So many descriptions of September 11, 2001, for example, begin with a remark about what a sunny morning it was.

Grief can make you feel like a sucker for having ever trusted in sunny days or all the basic givens of life, like health and safety and that people who matter to you will be here tomorrow. As C. S. Lewis explains it—also using the metaphor of a rope:

> It is easy to say you believe a rope to be strong and sound as long as you are using it to cord a box. But suppose you had to hang by that rope over a precipice. Wouldn't you discover how much you really trusted it?

Grief can feel like hanging over a precipice—the level of emotional vulnerability is that intense. So you have a natural wariness about grabbing hold of anything that seems iffy.

In these times of tragedy, when you are at your most sensitive about what words and gestures can be trusted, people will come at you with a tsunami of untrustworthy talk. You will be spoken to in clichés ("Time heals all wounds"), unsupportable assurances ("You're gonna get through this"), hokey cheer ("God took her 'cause he needed a new angel in heaven"), and even hokier solemnity ("It's all part of a larger plan"). Even professional people, from whom one would expect a higher level of "grief literacy," have shockingly mistaken notions about how to communicate with a grieving person. In Bill C. Davis's comic play *Mass Appeal,* a kindly parish priest with an affinity for sparkling burgundy dispenses "wisdom" on how to console. The scene is a fine example of how even professional consolers have flawed ideas about the way to talk with the grieving.

> Consolations *should* sound stupid so that the person in grief
> will realize how inconsolable their grief is. Inconsolable
> grief puts a person in a very exalted position. This feeling of
> being exalted gets most people through most tragedies. So
> your responsibility as a priest is to bring common grief to
> the heights of the inconsolable by saying something inane.

Occasionally a grieving person will call someone on the sort of bosh people speak—like the grieving father who said in response to a bromide about his young daughter who had died: "God took her because he needs another angel? He's God, why can't he *make* another angel?" While for the most part, this sort of untrustworthy language passes without comment, it still registers with someone in grief, even if only subconsciously. And it can affect your ability to trust.

You may find that you are not leaning on someone whom you thought would be a go-to person in a time of need. You may also find that you are inexplicably drawn to someone you never assumed you could trust. This scenario is quite common. You'll suddenly find yourself trusting a random co-worker over your best friend, a neighbor over your spouse, a cleaning lady over your shrink, a screw-up brother over the squeaky clean sister. It's because you are grabbing hold of the most solid rope you can find, even if it's being thrown to you by someone who may not love you as much as, or know you as well as, the person throwing you the looser line.

This can be painful for someone who wants you to trust him or lean on her, and such people will go to great lengths to get you to do so. "Catharsis stalkers," one person called them, meaning those people who always want you to "have a moment" with them, bare your heart, have a catharsis in their presence, *trust* them. The over-the-top ways in which these people try to win your trust will likely only make you shy away. Most people have an intuitive distrust of people who push too hard or in a way that's too extreme.

People who can be trusted are those who eschew the grand gesture. Their trustworthiness is apparent, usually because of how little they do to show it off. Mark Twain said, "A lie can travel halfway around the world while the truth is still putting on its shoes." Truth doesn't rush or try to make a fuss. It doesn't have to. Truthful words and gestures are always harbingers of trustworthiness, a good thing to bear in mind when debating with yourself whether you want to communicate with a particular person about your grief. The person who hires a high school marching band to play "Wind Beneath My Wings" on your front lawn in a formation that spells out TRUST ME may not be the ideal person to lean on.

You'll know the persons you can trust by observing how trustworthy they are in their smallest words and gestures, the most basic ropes they throw you. Again, this has nothing to do with who does or does not love you. It's just that the blend of honesty and compassion that distinguishes the trustworthy is hard to come by.

But it's out there.

In the movie *Wit* is a scene between Emma Thompson, playing a prominent British professor who's been stricken with terminal ovarian cancer, and Audra McDonald, playing an African-American nurse who cares for her. It's a masterly example of how to speak with someone who is in a difficult situation—whether dying or grieving.

Late one night the nurse walks into the scholar's hospital room and finds her fretting pensively—"having a wobble," as the English say. The stiff-upper-lipped scholar says, "I can't

seem to figure things out," and then her voice cracks with emotion. For many, the knee-jerk response to the sight of tears is,
"Oh, don't cry . . ." or, "It's going to be all right . . ." But the
nurse says directly, "What you're doing is very hard." Not a false
rope but one she has the other end of. It *is* hard. The nurse
knows it. All true.

Then the nurse goes face-to-face with the main elephant in
the room—she talks to the patient about her chemo-resistant
cancer. "It's like it's out of control, isn't it?" And at this invita-
tion to frankness, the scholar says (probably for the first time
in her life), "I'm scared." Again, a natural response might be to
toss a false rope to the patient, to say something like, "Don't be
scared . . ." or, "It'll be okay . . ." But the nurse says, "Of course
you are."

The scholar then begins castigating herself, saying, "I don't
feel sure of myself anymore." Still the nurse doesn't throw a
false rope, even though when suffering people launch into self-
recriminations we tend to throw all kinds of ropes we couldn't
possibly have the other end of. But the nurse just says, "You
used to feel sure, didn't you?"

Trust is beginning to form. The two of them then sit there, at
4 A.M., splitting one of those two-stick popsicles, talking as they
munch and slurp. Now that the patient knows she can trust
the ropes being thrown to her by the nurse, she communicates
more honestly:

SCHOLAR: My cancer's not being killed, is it?
NURSE: No. There isn't a good cure for what you have yet.
They should have explained this to you.
SCHOLAR: I knew.

Notice, Thompson's character already knows the worst of it.
This is the irony of the whole trust issue. People work so hard

to shield grieving people from things they already know. The scene ends with:

SCHOLAR: You're still going to take care of me, aren't you?
NURSE: Of course I am.

Even if the only solid rope you're offered is a popsicle and a promise of care, so be it. Small is okay. With grief, small promises that can be kept are better than big promises that can't. Your trust in the basic "okayness" of life will return bit by bit, as you try the smallest tugs on the rope. Trust rebuilds slowly, incrementally, and in a way that's diametrically opposed to the sudden, devastating way it crumbles when someone dies. The loss of trust feels "big," its return feels "small."

A widow who had lost her beloved husband was staying alone at a waterfront hotel on the one-year anniversary of his death. In the gift shop, perhaps looking a bit sad, she went to buy a bottle of water. An older woman at the cash register behind the counter said, "It's all right, dear. You can have it. No charge." The widow took the water and walked out of the shop. Then she stopped, suddenly aware of the small but solid rope that had just been thrown to her by a complete stranger. Although normally a reticent person, she went back in the shop and said to the cashier, "I just want to thank you for being kind that way. It made me feel good, and I needed some cheering up because I lost my husband a year ago today." The older lady replied, "In that case dear, you need some chocolate."

DENIAL

The song "I Get Along Without You Very Well" is a famous American standard, one of the great torch songs of the 1930s.

Many composers have called it "the saddest song ever written," and there's an interesting story behind its composition. The music was by Hoagy Carmichael, but the lyrics came from a poem someone had torn out of a newspaper and given to Carmichael. The poem was signed with the initials J.B. and had been sent to the newspaper anonymously. But Carmichael was so haunted by the bittersweet verse that he wrote a song using the poem as lyrics. He was so happy with it that he enlisted the help of some of the famous newspapermen of the day to find out who this mysterious J.B. was.

After much to-do the author was found: it was an elderly woman named Jane Brown Thompson. She was neither a poet nor a lyricist, and she never revealed to the public who or what the poem was about.

The song goes along saying, "I'll get along without you very well" *except* when this or that happens, like when "soft rain falls," or when the singer hears the name of the person who's gone away. In fact the song was originally called "I Get Along Without You Very Well (Except Sometimes)." That elaboration describes the point we wish to make about the issue of denial: *If you want to manage grief, be honest, open, frank, and real.* Except sometimes. Except about some things.

To people who have never experienced major grief, this may seem like a contradiction to much of what we have already said in this chapter. But if you have experienced major grief, you will know that it is not so much a contradiction as it is a paradox. Yes, it's important to process all aspects of grief honestly, to stare them square in the face; but there will often be at least one place in the heart or mind about which you will conclude, "Let's not go there." This is where the song comes in. It is the last lines that make the song so sad.

> I get along without you very well
> Except, of course, in Spring.

But I will never think of Spring,
For that would surely break my heart in two.

The singer won't think of Spring. Ever. There are places too ten-der for some people to go—even in a torch song. So they never will, and that's that. And this is fine. Some things need not be faced overtly, and if that's your choice it doesn't mean that you are in . . . (here comes that word) . . . *denial.*

One of the most aggravating things you can hear is when someone accuses you of being in "denial." People toss this word around far too much, and do so as if they were experts. A psy-chologist we spoke with told a story about a co-worker who had died the day before. When the psychologist wandered down to the main office to see how people were doing, a secretary immediately pulled him aside and said, "They're not taking it well. Everyone is in denial, and I happen to know that's the first stage of grief." To which the psychologist replied, "Well, maybe you'll help them achieve 'Anger' by the end of the day." The point is, just because you're not sharing your feelings doesn't mean that you're in the "denial" others so freely diagnose.

No one could accuse Suse Lowenstein of being in denial. People in denial don't spend fifteen years of their life sculpting seventy-six women reenacting the most devastating moment of their lives. But one of the first things Suse said when we sat down to talk was, "I happen to be a great believer in denial. . . . You can't do it all at once. It's just too much." This sort of benign denial isn't about "avoiding" the issue altogether, it's about pac-ing yourself through certain aspects of grief. Grief is a lot to pro-cess in one batch, so your mind may try to slow the process and take things as you are ready for them, almost prioritizing them. You don't have to speed home from the hospice the day your loved one has died and make a spread-sheet of all the terrible moments you'll need to sort through. There's no need to rush.

Many people choose to handle their grief in manageable units. They may confront a certain aspect of grief as if it were a pending household chore, a tough project that can't be confronted until one is ready to roll up one's sleeves and get to work on it. It's the emotional version of, "This summer, come hell or high water, I'm buying storage boxes at Home Depot and organizing that pigsty of a basement." Some people will literally think to themselves, "Pretty soon I'll be ready to start talking about how angry I felt at dad in his last few months."

Grieving is hard work. You need time between stretches of that work to catch your breath and recharge yourself. Denial can be that necessary rest, and a healthy rest at that. A cartoon in *The New Yorker* shows two women walking down the street. One turns to the other and says, "I'm feeling much better now that I'm back in denial."

Pacing yourself as you process grief is not denial. If, after twenty-five years, you're still setting a place at the dinner table for your loved one who died—okay, that's denial. But there is plenty of wiggle room between being a grief masochist who does too much, too soon, and being someone so lost in denial that you take up residence in the attic. It is not only healthy for you to set *your own* timetable for processing aspects of your grief; it is also one of the only areas of grieving over which you have some autonomy.

I'll do it when I'm damn good and ready.

Aside from *when* you choose to "deal," it's also right for you to choose *what* facets to deal with and what facets you may never wish to deal with. You are not necessarily in denial if there are a few horrors you prefer to keep locked away *always.* You can just say, "I just don't want to go there." In the case of some of the more overwhelming images or aspects of a loss, it's not so much that you "don't want to go there," it's that you may *already* be there. You know you have some buttons that shouldn't be pushed. Maybe it's because they are overwhelming. Maybe it's because they are sacred and need to stay in a chamber of the mind or heart that's off-limits, even to yourself. Some of these things too painful to deal with are, in many cases, not even essential for maintaining an honest approach to grief.

For example, one thing people don't wish to dwell on is a common occurrence: the uncharacteristically awful way that some dying people treat others around them. The kindest, warmest of people will, under the reality of their impending death, snap at their family, lash out at friends, and in many ways be completely dreadful to be around.

There is no need to turn these outbursts over and over in your mind. They are not what the person was, only what they were when overtaken by pain. Our human reaction to pain is involuntary. Close your finger in the car door and you'll shriek like hell. You can't help it. When you are sick enough, it feels like your whole body is being closed in a car door. Elizabeth Kubler-Ross, the doctor who first developed the Five Stages of Grief, explains, ". . . Anger is displaced in all directions and projected onto the environment at times almost at random. . . . Wherever the patient looks at this time, he will find grievances."

You are not in denial if you don't wish to rehash lurid scenes of being on the receiving end of a pain-crazed person's venom in the last days of a life. If you have experienced this sort of thing, people may seek to console you by tsk-tsking, "They always turn on the people they love the most"—a statement that is scarcely consoling. Grieving is meant to be a process of recovery; it is not a self-flagellating ritual you owe to the dead.

Nor are you "in denial" if there are images you do not wish to replay. These images have to do not only with the loved one who died but may extend to those still around. When a loved one dies, you often find yourself in a room with other people you love, watching them suffer as well. This can be a lot to process, and you may choose not to. A young man who lost his sister in the Continental Airlines plane crash in Buffalo, New

York, in February 2009, said after calling home, "I heard my mother make a noise on the phone I have never heard before." We heard similar remarks from others. How many times have you heard someone say, "The only time I ever saw them cry was at so-and-so's funeral." Grief can bring out responses in those closest to you that you may just not care to relive. And what would be the point? It happened. You saw it or heard it. There's no reason to relive it. Honesty need not be torture.

A final note about the lady who wrote "I Get Along Without You Very Well." After discovering the identity of Jane Thompson, Hoagy Carmichael hired the popular singer Dick Powell to debut the song on a radio program. The day before the show aired, Jane Thompson died.

Maybe she just didn't want to go there.

MISTAKES

Grief can be a minefield. For someone in grief, and for those trying to support that person, hidden emotional bombs are everywhere. They're easy to step on and, when detonated, can really do damage.

The concept of the mistake is one of the most human issues related to grief. Very few mistakes that occur during grief happen because people are malicious. Emotionally frazzled, yes. In the dark on certain issues, yes. Flat-out dumb sometimes, yes. But usually there's no malice. There's a reason why one of the most common adjectives used to qualify the word "mistake" is "honest"—as in, "it was an *honest* mistake." Most mistakes made at a time of grief, either by the grieving person or by those within the grieving person's circle, are honest mistakes.

This is part of what makes the issue so hard to sort out, and frankly, so sad. Even though mistakes made during grief may be honest, because they occur at a time when you are exposed and highly sensitive to pain, they can still hurt badly.

David Lindsay Abaire's play *Rabbit Hole* is the story of a young, married couple who lose their only child, Danny, age four. While chasing after the family dog, Danny runs into the street and is hit by a car—right in front of the family's house. The play takes place in the months after Danny's death as the couple struggles to find their way forward in life. In one scene the husband picks up a VCR tape and discovers that a horrible mistake has been made. His wife has recorded a documentary about tornadoes from the Discovery Channel, but the tape she used had contained the last footage of their son alive. It has been erased for good.

The incident was an unfortunate cluster of honest mistakes. The wife was taping the show for her husband, trying to give his anguished mind a half-hour of relief by absorbing it in something besides the endless loop of Danny's death. The husband wasn't being thoughtless either. He couldn't sleep the night before (the infamous 4:30 A.M. perhaps?), so rather than wake his wife he probably went downstairs, watched the tape of Danny, had a good cry into a throw pillow so his wife wouldn't hear him, and then staggered back to bed, leaving the tape in the machine.

Still, as honest as these mistakes are, it doesn't change the fact that the footage of Danny is gone forever. Los Angeles Lakers' announcer Chick Hearn coined the famous phrase, "No harm, no foul." Were he doing play-by-play of the arguments that loved ones have over mistakes made in times of grief, he could have said, "No foul, still harm."

A mistake can feel so hurtful to the person on the receiving end of it that he or she can't help but think there was some darker motive in the mind of the offender. In thinking this way, you may allow honest mistakes to become what T. S. Eliot called an "objective correlative." This is when, in Eliot's words, "a set of objects, a situation, a chain of events" become "a formula for that particular emotion." In *Rabbit Hole* the erased tape becomes the *object* that the father *correlates* to the death of Danny as a means of letting loose his feelings. He can't have a knock-down-drag-out fight with the thoughtless mistake of Danny running into the street and being killed; there is no such monster for him to get his mitts on. What he *can* get his mitts on is the thoughtless mistake that took away the taped footage of Danny. *That* is standing right in front of him in the living room in the person of his wife and her honest mistake.

At a time of grief there are all sorts of what Eliot calls "formulas" for the volatile emotions floating around, and they're just looking for an object, a situation, or a person they can use as ingredients to cook up an explosion.

For example, we heard a story about a woman who lost her husband. On the day of his funeral she was supposed to pick her mother up at the airport on the way to the church. But she forgot. She left her mother at the airport and went off to the church without her. The mother missed her son-in-law's funeral and spent three hours wandering around baggage claim. One has to wonder how someone could make such a big mistake, could leave her mother pacing around an airport thinking, "Well, guess who's an objective correlative today?"

But if you are in grief your mind is not working the way it normally does. How could it? The most elemental logic has been skewed: a loved one who has always been there is gone. The brain can't compute this, so there is a temporary insanity. Grieving people rarely describe early grief as "sad" but rather as "surreal," "like a bad dream," "the sensation of shock."

Grief is really a kind of derangement, and "derangement: comes from a root meaning "not in place." The grieving person's mind is working overtime to compute why someone who has always been there is not in his or her place. Danny is out of place; the husband of the woman who left her mother at the airport is out of place. Why shouldn't grieving people's thoughts be out of place for a while?

During grief your mind is compromised. Emotionally you are an exposed nerve. The small bumps and grinds of insensitivity that most people deal with on a normal basis may feel not only like mistakes but cruel. We heard a story about two parents whose sixteen-year-old son was killed by a drunk driver over a long weekend. The following Monday the grief-besotted parents received a prerecorded voicemail from the school district informing them that their child "was not in school today." The recording went on to enumerate the school's policy on unexcused absences. They received the same message for the next three days.

Of course this is terrible, but the recording was merely the school district's efficient system for notifying parents when their child was not in class. Although that probably didn't matter to the poor couple who kept getting the message. "No foul, still harm."

When the school's administrators, most of whom were parents themselves, realized their mistake, they were appalled. They apologized, and the removal of a deceased student's name from the automated absence notification system is now done immediately.

You may feel a particular gall about these types of mistakes made by large entities—a company, an agency, a school district. Grieving people can come to loath faceless institutions. Many people in grief spend torturous hours on the phone with a bank, a government office, or even the (expletive) cable company. Already emotionally exhausted, you may turn blue in the face trying to get the bureaucratic automaton on the other end of the line to understand that the "party" about whom they're speaking is dead and thus in no position to do thus-and-such "within the next thirty days to avoid fees." And can we please pass a law making it illegal for these people to end a call that has made a grieving person pull out tufts of hair by saying, "Have a nice day"?

A great Leviathan of a corporation or institution is easy to view as an evil phantom, and many companies or agencies seem to go out of their way to live up to the billing. But there is a big difference in the mistakes made by people who are trying to support you if you are grieving. Your predisposition will be to forgive mistakes these people make. You have already lost someone, so the ranks of your "loved ones" have thinned. You want to hold on to everyone you still have.

Strangely, though, this is the exact opposite of how you may be approached by others. People can be, odd as this may sound, *intimidated* by someone in grief. They sometimes look at you as if you were a minor celebrity, as if some strange aura of ennobling grief were emanating from you. This terrifies some people that they may make a mistake, saying or doing the wrong thing.

So, of course, they do.

Gertrude Stein expressed this tendency in her typically paradoxical phraseology, "Everybody knows if you are too careful, you are so preoccupied being careful, that you are sure to stumble."

In a famous episode of *All in the Family*, Sammy Davis, Jr., comes to the Bunker household because he left his attaché case in Archie's cab. Archie, a domineering know-it-all, tells his family that Davis has a glass eye (which he did in real life, a fact that was common knowledge). Archie warns everyone to be careful not to say anything awkward about it. Davis arrives and during the visit is offered coffee. Archie, playing the gracious host, hands him a cup of coffee and, as he does, looks Davis right in the face and says, "Do you take cream and sugar in your eye?"

These kinds of tongue slips happen all the time, but they tend to be worse for the Archies of the world than the Sammy Davis, Jr.'s, worse for the tongue slipper than the grieving person.

People talking to someone in grief think if they accidentally say the word "cancer," or the name of the street on which the accident happened, or the name of the person who died, or (a biggie) the word "death" in any form or context, they have made a huge mistake. They'll say something like, "I was late for work because my battery died," then suddenly turn purple at having said the D-word. But this is an irrational fear and an unnecessary caution. If you are in grief you know your lost loved one's name, know he or she died and will stay dead. You live with that fact, writ large, every day of your life. Chances are you're not going to turn on someone who uses the D-word and say, "Your *battery* died? Well, so did my husband, bitch!"

Still, people feel ill at ease, and when they do make a mistake, the instinct is to try to hide their awkwardness and act like it didn't happen, even when everyone clearly knows it did. Of course this only makes things more awkward. Watching someone try to hide their discomfort makes a griever feel worse. If someone makes a mistake around you, talk about it—lightly and dismissively of course, but bring it up. Say, "No big deal," and move on.

The *New York Times* reported on a study which showed that patients are far less likely to sue doctors who make mistakes if those doctors are candid about how they erred, and if the injured patient "receives an honest explanation, an apology, and prompt, fair compensation for the harm they have suffered." Statistics proving that patients who receive an apology are less likely to sue have been so compelling that "more than 30 states have enacted laws making apologies for medical errors inadmissible in court." In the past, "many doctors had been afraid that admitting and describing their errors would only invite a law-suit," but the reverse is true.

This study says a lot about more than medicine. It tells us something about the way human beings are wired when it comes to what we really want from people who have hurt us. We want sincere understanding, not retribution. For most people, an ounce of honesty is more valuable than a pound of flesh.

SENTIMENTALITY

For years scholars and critics have argued about what exactly is troubling Hamlet, the most overdiscussed dramatic character in history. Of course, if anyone had asked Hamlet himself, he could have told them what's eating him, at least when we first meet him in Act I, because he says so in no uncertain terms. Hamlet is boiling because, shortly after his father's suspicious death, his mother has already remarried his dead father's brother. But equally as galling for Hamlet, his mother, Queen Gertrude, made an emotional spectacle of herself at his father's funeral, a spectacle that was, in Hamlet's mind, appallingly dishonest. He smolders at the image of her, following his "poor father's body . . . like Niobe—all tears." This funeral performance felt to Hamlet as though "the salt of most unrighteous tears" cried by his mother were being poured into the open wound of his more authentic grief.

This is a "wound" and a "salt" that many people in grief will recognize. You may be hurt by the emotions of others when they appear tainted by narcissism and insincerity. Around any death there will always be people who use the situation for their own purposes, people who turn the sacred and communal experience of grief into a personal agenda. This may manifest itself in a display that makes someone with more authentic grief wince. There is a dividing line between those who engage in "grief shtick" and those whose grief is more genuine. The former behavior is what we call "sentimentality," and in Hamlet's first speech he nails it to the wall. When his mother accuses him of "seeming" to grieve too much for his dead father, Hamlet lets her have it:

> Seems, Madam? Nay, it is. I know not "seems."
> 'Tis not alone my inky cloak, good mother,
> Nor customary suits of solemn black,
> Nor windy suspiration of forc'd breath,
> No, nor the fruitful river in the eye,
> Nor the dejected haviour of the visage,
> Together with all forms, moods, shapes of grief,
> That can denote me truly. These indeed seem,
> For they are actions that a man might show,
> These but the trappings and the suits of woe.

This issue is as true today as it was for Hamlet. While it is an awkward subject to talk about, it is a kind of behavior that makes grieving people seethe. You may be deeply troubled by someone who seems to grieve but is really indulging in the emotion of the situation with a self-serving relish. Most grieving people keep quiet about it, but if you give them license to talk about the issue they'll give you an earful.

An amusing example of this sort of thing can be found in Lanford Wilson's play *The Fifth of July*. The character of a plucky and eccentric seventy-year-old woman named Sally Talley goes to the funeral of her beau from fifty years earlier. She confronts one of these "seemers," and the rage she feels almost makes her faint.

> I was sitting there listening to that stupid Reverend Poole,
> and looked over at that smug wife of his, always so pleased

to have an occasion to show how easily she can cry. She was like that in school. You'd say, Francine, cry! And she'd burst into tears for you.

We have all known "Francine Pooles" (or "Frank Pooles"). They can be spotted in any grieving situation, and just about everyone present will know who they are.

At a time of tragedy you are so preoccupied with your own grief that you can ignore the one person who is cheapening the occasion. And most people feel that it's uncharitable to pass judgment on another person's behavior at such an emotionally fraught time. But the anger is there. And justifiable. This is not about being proprietary about your emotional claim on the dead; it's rather about respect for your loved one. You may not like watching these sentimental "seemers" (as Hamlet would call them) cash in on the death of your loved one, embezzling the feelings surrounding that death for their own emotional and egotistical booty.

While it may sound crass to talk about sentiment in such monetary terms, it is the most common metaphor used in describing sentimentality, both in literature and in descriptions from grieving people. James Joyce called sentimentality "unearned emotion." Oscar Wilde used a similar metaphor when he defined a sentimentalist as "one who desires to have the luxury of emotion without having to pay for it." In Act V of *Hamlet*, at Ophelia's funeral, Hamlet comes out of hiding and says, "I loved Ophelia. Forty-thousand brothers could not with all their quantity of love make up my sum."

This "value" imagery is apt. We all know the particular "sum" of love that existed between us and our loved one. Sentimentalists co-opt more of the deceased person than they are due, and this can have a hurtful effect on those who are more truly stricken by the death.

A college grief counselor we spoke to said that in any grieving situation involving students he always looks at the "margins
of the scene," because that is often where he finds the person
who is hurting most, sitting away from the group, yielding center stage to the filchers of sentiment, too hurt to engage in what
Hamlet calls "actions that a man might show."

We saw this exact paradigm play out on a college campus
in Long Island, New York. A popular boy had died suddenly. A
crowd gathered at a makeshift memorial ablaze with candles
and snapshots. The person in the crowd who knew the boy
best was not the girl for whom the paramedics had to be called.
She, it turned out, had known the dead student only a few
months, having "been in a play with him." (*Windy suspirations
of forced breath.*) Nor was it the fellow who was (unasked) playing his guitar, strumming loudly. The student who was hurting, bone-deep, was the boy's roommate and great friend. He
was sitting off to the side alone, "on the margins," too crushed
to be in the center of the scene.

Excessive emotion does not necessarily indicate sentimentality in the pejorative way we use the term. Some people are
highly emotional, and their hair-trigger lachrymal glands are
about real feeling, not false sentiment. We all know and love
people like this. (You may even be one.) They are warmhearted,
genuine, and seek no special attention. And we never mind
their easy emotion at a time of grief. We have seen them cry
over Christmas music, dog-food commercials, kind thank-you
notes, or a guy popping the question on the JumboTron during *Monday Night Football*. These people are not sentimentalists
because *they* "have that within that passeth show."

Sentimentalism, on the other hand, thrives on "show." What
sentimentalists feel is less important than *that* they feel it. They
need to have their emotion legitimized by having other people
see it. This is why it's common to see a sentimentalist hijack a

memorial service. In Christopher Buckley's memoir about his parents' deaths he skewers these funeral stealers:

> You have probably attended one or two memorial services where the fine-hammered steel of woe was turned to Brillo by incontinent eulogists. This species can be easily spotted: they almost never prepare ahead of time, preferring instead to "go with the moment" or to "speak from the heart." They will prattle on—from the heart—for at least twenty minutes, causing those in attendance to forget all about the deceased and start praying that a dislodged gargoyle will fall from above and smite the speaker.

Buckley gave every speaker at his father's funeral four minutes, and told them all, "I have snipers positioned."

If you are grieving, you'll also have to wrestle with your own sentimentality. It's common for someone sitting down to write an obituary, a eulogy, or some sort of memorial to fall into the prefabricated words and phrases of the sentimentalist.

We tend to be a sentimental culture. Sentiment sells, and there is, consequently, an abundance of it floating around. It affects us all. Be aware that sentiment and respect are opposite sides of the same coin. Like sentiment, respect is a valuation of the person. We "*pay* our respects," to someone, or we "owe it to them." But where sentiment uses the value of the deceased for the emotional needs of others, respect is about giving someone their honest due.

Some people feel that the way to pay respect to someone is by using hyperbole and plenty of grandiose sentiment. This usually ends up obliterating the unique nature of an individual rather than distinguishing the person.

We saw an eleven-year-old at the funeral of his grandmother give a superb example of how to do it, swimming against the tide of adult self-indulgence. They had come to the part in the service where anyone who wishes may come to the front of the chapel and say something about the deceased—a ritual that can sometimes turn into a jamboree of self-absorbed sentimentality and unintentional disrespect to the dead.

Several members of this particular family spoke—interrupted periodically by people's cell phones going off. All of them gushed on and on about how the deceased woman had helped *them* with *their* problems, saved *them*, supported *them*, rehabbed *them*, got *them* through dysfunctional love relationships, believed in *them*, fed *them*, loved *them*, and had been there for *them* through thick and thin. In a few instances the dead woman hadn't done quite enough for the speaker, who nonetheless was now willing publicly to forgive her.

Then her eleven-year-old grandson rose to talk. He didn't say a word about himself. He spoke only of his grandmother—how she had come to America as an immigrant with nothing and made her way, and raised a family, and worked hard, and loved much, and been a fine lady. In the most genuine terms, the boy described all he had observed and admired about his grandmother and now saw fit to honor. He put a roomful of adults to shame. And he ended by saying, "And turn off your cell phones so you don't look like jackasses."

A small masterstroke of respect.

Respect for the dead is not about adopting a gushing attitude. It is about letting us know who a person honestly was. Here is an excerpt from a paid obituary placed in a newspaper:

> You were the best mother in the entire world. No son has ever been more loved. You were the greatest, kindest, most wonderful person imaginable. An incomparable spirit.

When you first read this, it seems like a perfectly loving and respectful tribute. But a closer look shows two things. First, it's a tribute that could apply to just about any mother on earth except Joan Crawford. There is nothing that distinguishes the woman, gives us a sense of her, lets us *see* her. Second, and the most common trap for people writing tributes to a loved one, is that it's all from the perspective of how the son feels at the over-wrought time he is writing. A few years down the line, when the heat of sentiment cools, as it always does, this obituary will seem stale and awash in a million others just like it.

Compare it with one from a local paper in northern California: "She loved her family. She loved teaching. She loved gardening." They're simple words, but you get a clearer picture of the woman.

When you write something about a loved one who has died, shy away from the hyperboles used in the first obituary—"best," "ever," "most," "imaginable," "entire world," and especially the big ones like "incomparable" and "extraordinary." Concentrate on respect and honesty. Words that will stand the test of time are not gushing but true. Don't aim for grandiosity; instead pursue the small and telling stroke, the bull's-eye detail.

A few favorites. The first comes from the "In Memoriam" section of the *New York Times* and is for a woman born in 1908 who died in 2006: "Dear Bess, I walked the beaches of Grayland without you for the first time last Sunday—missing you, a babe to the end in your bright orange sweater. Love, Tom." The tribute says nothing about Tom, except how much he loved Bess. But can't you just picture this woman? Ninety-eight, still beach strolling, still stylish.

Another favorite comes from the *Arizona Republic*. It's about a man who worked at a meatpacking plant. His family writes: "If you want to do something in his memory: Go out and have a big steak and tip your hat to all the country's beef producers—he would like that."

A few days later a letter was sent to the paper in response. A man from Sun City West wrote back: "I'd like Mr. Vincent's family to know that I shall soon do exactly that, and raise a forkful (rare, of course) to that cattleman's accomplishments." It's hard to do much better than having a complete stranger write to the paper about your tribute.

Using familiar words makes the person you are writing about *feel* more familiar. It keeps you from trying to make him something he wasn't. It keeps you honestly respectful. This is Senator Ted Kennedy at the funeral of his brother Bobby:

> My brother need not be idealized or enlarged in death beyond who he was in life. To be remembered simply as a good and decent man, who saw wrong and tried to right it, saw suffering and tried to heal it, saw war and tried to stop it. Those of us who loved him, and who take him to his rest today, pray that what he was and what he wished for others will someday come to pass for all the world. As he said many times, in many parts of this nation, to those he touched and who sought to touch him: "Some men see things as they are and say, 'Why?' I dream things that never were and say, 'Why not?'"

One hundred twenty-four words, and 109 of them one syllable. Simple, respectful, true, and much more moving than a flood of sentimental boilerplate. This is the eloquence of honesty. The sentimentalists don't know what they're missing.

HUMOR

In a Russian shtetl two men, Moshe and Yankel, are about to be shot by a firing squad of marauding Cossacks. As one of them puts a blindfold on Yankel, he spits in the soldier's face and sneers, "You dirty Cossack bastard!" Moshe turns to him and in hushed tones says, "Please, Yankel—don't make trouble."

No situation is so grave that some people won't tell a joke about it, and no situation is so grave that some people won't tell a joke *during* it.

Humor's ability to alleviate suffering has been a popular topic of medical discussion ever since Norman Cousins's groundbreaking book, *Anatomy of an Illness*. Cousins, who eventually received a professorship in the UCLA School of Medicine, chronicled his personal experience with a horrific degenerative illness during which he used humor (Cousins called it "inner jogging") to relieve his pain and eventually heal himself. He would watch Marx Brothers movies because he found that "ten minutes of genuine belly laughter" would give him "two hours of pain-free sleep."

The curative powers of humor have now become an accepted fact, and the *Duck Soup for the Soul* gospel is everywhere in our culture. "Laughter is the best medicine" is both a common adage and a popular feature in *Reader's Digest*, and for the past fifty years the American family refrigerator has had at least one "how to cope with trouble" anecdote or cartoon stuck to it. Hollywood too has jumped on the "healing power of humor" bandwagon, each year turning out some variation on the theme of the renegade funnyman who brings the curative powers of humor to the downtrodden or ill.

But while humor in healing is well understood, people are at a loss about its role in grief. Very few individuals are comfortable using humor in a grieving situation. They fear it's inappropriate and have thus stamped it as taboo. Grieving situations are allowed to remain unremittingly bleak, with not so much as a snicker to break the gloom, leaving the field open only to those who use humor poorly and at the wrong time. Uncle Al telling knock-knock jokes at shivah is not a welcome presence.

Humor is the same as other instinctual responses to trouble in that it divides along the lines of *flight* or *fight*. Faced with peril, humans either try to escape (flight) or they stay to duke it out (fight). The same is true for the coping mechanism of humor. There is "flight humor" and "fight humor." Flight humor seeks to escape your troubles, tries to get your mind off your pain, as the Marx Brothers movies did for Norman Cousins. With fight humor, on the other hand, you aren't trying to escape. You're staying to confront whatever is wrong. Fight humor doesn't take your mind off the problem, it puts your mind on it. It calls the trouble out in order to help you deal with the things you *can't* take your mind off.

When it comes to grief, fight humor is much more helpful.

Eventually you may find yourself able to take flight from your feelings of grief by getting lost in a silly TV comedy or a movie. In the early stages of grief, however, the escapism of flight humor is not only impossible, it's infuriating. A common sensation that grieving people talk about is a feeling of inexplicable rage toward the rest of the world that seems to be blithely going about its happy business while your personal world has tipped on its axis. W. H. Auden's "Funeral Blues" is probably the best-known modern poem on the subject of grief, and the reason it strikes such a chord with grieving people is because of how well it vents this aggravation:

> Stop all the clocks, cut off the telephone,
> Prevent the dog from barking with a juicy bone. . .
> The stars are not wanted now: put out every one;
> Pack up the moon and dismantle the sun. . .

If you're feeling like you want the clocks and the stars to cease, the good-natured fun of escapist comedy will play like nails on a chalkboard. You're not in the mood for a can of silly string.

Flight humor—escapist fun—may bring relief to people who are ill, but there is a great difference between illness and grief. The pain of illness comes from the body. Take your mind off the pain and it can be alleviated. But the pain of grief comes from love, and love can't be alleviated. In illness there is always hope for healing, even if it's hope for a last-minute miracle. There is no healing grief. The person is gone, and that fact won't ever change. As Groucho Marx, Cousins's salvation, once quipped: "Time wounds all heels." Sometimes it feels to the griever that time wounds all *heals*. Grieving people understand this fact very quickly. Hours after someone dies, you begin feeling the finality you are up against. You know you can't fly away from reality, it's here to stay. So any tool you use to survive has to be one that helps you wrestle with your new reality.

This is where *fight* humor comes in.

Humor can be used to fight with these darkest feelings. Sigmund Freud wrote a whole book on the subject called *Jokes and Their Relation to the Unconscious*. Freud (who was not known as a particularly hilarious person) recognized humor as a profound and effective means of battling despair. He saw jokes as an avenue by which the forbidden thoughts and feelings suppressed by society might surface. In words that sound like a battle cry, Freud calls humor "an attitude by means of which a person refuses to suffer, emphasizes the invincibility of his ego, victoriously maintains his pleasure principle."

Grief wields such power over a person that it can begin to feel like God, and at times stronger than God. Humor is one way to take this giant down a peg or two, to disempower it, to undercut its dark dignity by slamming it with a pie.

If fight humor is about letting you say what you really feel, the following story we heard from an East Coast family is a perfect example. They had lost their father a few days earlier and were sitting around the kitchen table on the morning of his wake. The widowed mother and her three high-school-age children were silently picking at breakfast, being turned inside-out at the thought of having to walk into the funeral home and see, for the first time, their father laid out dead in a casket. The scene was tense and miserable. But then the oldest daughter walked into the kitchen and exclaimed in a loud, sarcastic voice, "Well, Happy Fucking We're Going to a Wake Day!" The siblings and the mother almost choked on their coffee, it was so shocking and so funny to them. The "forbidden" was made conscious, and the family laughed.

Her comment helped because it was fight humor. If she had walked into the kitchen and said, "Hey, did you hear the one about . . . ," it would have been flight humor, and probably would have come off as awkward and forced, making the situation even more uncomfortable. But the daughter didn't walk around the ick; she walked through it. Sometimes a little bad behavior is just what the doctor ordered.

It can be awful how well you are expected to behave in the face of grief, and humor is one of the only things you may have to remind yourself that there is a world, even joy, outside the all-encompassing vacuum of grieving. In a scene in Shakespeare's *Twelfth Night*, the puritanical fusspot Malvolio storms into a midnight party being held by a character whose name pretty much sums up his personality—Sir Toby Belch. Malvolio tries to stop the raucous fun, but the tipsy Belch replies with one of the great lines in all comic literature: "Dost thou think, because thou art virtuous, there shall be no more cakes and ale?"

Few things are more filled with virtue than those stiff, postmortem days of wake, funeral, shivah, and so forth. Everyone holds the door for others, says polite things in muted tones, and dutifully adheres to all the solemnity, formality, and protocol that the deceased person would find ridiculous. With all this virtuousness going on, it's okay to look for a few comic targets at which to aim a little fight humor. They are usually plentiful. There are undertakers who give people the heebie-jeebies as they hover around; there are priests, rabbis, and preachers who have strange vocal ticks or strange hair, and frequently both;

and there is usually at least one unquestionably awful person you will have to deal with, like the lady who rules over the church organ with the vigilance of a navy SEAL and the singing voice of a real seal. If all else fails, there will always be relatives you haven't seen in a while whom time has not been good to. Remember that humor isn't something you can manufacture at will, it's something that just happens. You don't make humor; you allow it. So don't Google "grief jokes" to see what zingers you can find. Merely allow and share the humor that falls from above. And it usually does.

People aren't sure when it's okay to begin laughing again. A rule of thumb is something the brilliant comic writer Larry Gelbart once said. A woman at a cocktail party had asked him, "Why does everyone take an instant dislike to me?" Gelbart replied, "It saves time." That's how you should feel about fight humor: do it today, it saves time. If you can say, "Someday we'll laugh about this," you should be able to laugh about it then and there. "Someday" you won't need it as much as you do today. Alan Alda told a story about Gelbart having to leave a funeral, oddly enough, to go to another funeral. As he got up to exit, he said to the assembled mourners, "Sorry, I hate to grieve and run." Gelbart wasn't waiting for "someday" when he made this crack. He knew that fight humor has the most value when it's used in the moment.

When Graham Chapman, one of the founding members of Monty Python, died of a rare cancer at age forty-eight, a surviving member of the comedy troupe couldn't even wait until after his funeral to begin using fight humor. Chapman's sudden death happened on the eve of the twentieth anniversary of the first episode of *Flying Circus*. Fellow Python Terry Jones called it "the worst case of party-pooping in all history." John Cleese, who was with Chapman when he died and became so upset that he had to leave the room, also felt a need to fight the gloom. This is part of the eulogy he gave for his departed friend of twenty years.

> I guess that we're all thinking how sad it is that a man of such talent, of such capability and kindness, of such unusual intelligence, should now, so suddenly, be spirited away at the age of only forty-eight, before he'd achieved many of the things of which he was capable and before he'd had enough fun. Well, I feel that I should say: *Nonsense! Good riddance to him, the free-loading bastard, I hope he fries!* And the reason I feel I should say this, is he would never forgive me if I didn't, if I threw away this glorious opportunity to shock you all on his behalf. Anything for him but mindless good taste. I could hear him whispering in my ear last night as I was writing this, "Alright, Cleese," he was saying, "you're very proud of being the very first person ever to say 'shit' on British television. If this service is really for me, just for starters, I want you to become the first person ever at a British memorial service to say 'Fuck.'"

The assembled mourners were, naturally, convulsed—either in laughter or shock or (best of all) both!

In the middle of the storm of sadness, people need to be reminded of certain things. There will be humor again. There will be life. Clocks will once again tick and stars will be wanted. And in the fight against the smothering virtue of grief, there will be cakes and ale.

CHAPTER THREE

THE NINE CONSOLATIONS

REST

Simple rest is one of the most effective remedies for the pain of grief. It is also one of the hardest things to get a grieving person to do. Grieving people can be their own worst taskmasters. They can be overly driven, telling themselves that it may be "fine for other people to rest," but "I can't because *I* have too much to do."

Albert Camus scratched the following three sentences in one of his journals:

Stages of healing.
Let volition sleep.
Enough of "you must."

While these notes were written only for himself, to maintain his peace of mind during a hard time, they are a simple, spot-on anthem for the consolation of rest. The very first stage of healing is to let volition sleep, to take that interior voice that keeps saying "You must! You must! You must!" and tell it to back off. Simply say, "Enough."

The mental chorus of "You must!" that Camus identifies is not an easy thing to shut off. Much of it comes from the forceful

white noise of our culture. We're a country that thrives on volition, and we are inundated daily with messages telling us that
being "always on the go" is our highest cultural good. One need
only look at TV commercials, every other one of which seems to
end the same way. After Metamucil has made the man regular
or Paxil has made the woman sane, the happy ending always
shows the person hoisting a grandchild into the air at the town
fair or giving a thumbs-up to the camera as she windsurfs by.
"Always on the go"—the ultimate American confirmation that
we are "a-ok."

This implies that if we are *not* on the go, something is wrong
with us. Rest is viewed as being almost seditious, and the person in need of it is thought of as slightly suspect. Tell people
you can't see them Friday night because you've got a kickbox-
ing tournament and they'll think you're a terrific person. Tell
them you can't see them Friday night because you need some
quiet time and they'll think you're a mental case—or, at the
very least, that "something is *wrong.*"

You may sense this cultural taboo and fight hard not to be
tainted by it. Because of your loss, you may already feel alienated from the stream of "normal life," so you are reluctant to
succumb to the need for rest because you fear it will make you
seem even more "out of it." So you make a Herculean effort to
keep going, unaware of the phenomenal drain on your energy
from the particulars of grief. This is the exact opposite of what
you should do.

If you are a grieving person, this is where the Camus mantra
comes in. Even though it may be hard, you must allow yourself
that first stage of restful healing. For example, you may not like
to think of yourself as the kind of person who has outside help
come in to clean. Too bad. For a few months, hire someone.
You may pride yourself on being the kind of person who always
mows his own lawn. Too bad. Get a neighbor's kid to do it for a

while. And here's the clincher: when the cleaning lady vacuums poorly and the lawn boy decapitates a few daffodils, *let volition sleep, enough of "you must."*

Grieving is such an all-encompassing experience that you may not be aware of how much "juice" it burns up. It's as if someone came along and, unbeknownst to you, hooked up a massive appliance in your basement that's using tons more wattage than you realize. You're being drained in more ways than you know.

For one thing, you may become so used to being over-whelmed with emotion, you forget what a taxing experience emotion itself can be, how deep the feelings are. And how phys-ical. Is it ever possible to talk about experiencing big emotions without using the word "gut" in the description? People forget how abnormal it is to go through that sort of upheaval time and time again, as grieving people regularly do.

The nongrieving woman leaves the door to the bathroom open during her morning shower so she can listen to the TV news. The grieving woman shuts the door so the children can't hear her sob in the one private place she knows she can go to. Which person emerges from the shower more drained? This happens so often that the grieving person almost gets used to it. She forgets what a debilitating phenomenon strong emotion is. If the woman cried on a street corner as she does each morning in the shower, jaws would drop, dogs would bark, and passersby would call paramedics. But for a grieving person that sort of thing is just "a day in the life."

It's remarkable how tiring emotion is compared with almost any other kind of effort, no matter how tough. You can bounce back from the physical exertion of running a ten-kilometer race or the mental exertion of doing your taxes after one good night's sleep. But you can't do that after the sort of exertion caused by emotion. Even a small dose of it, like the kind you feel over a spat with your spouse, or receiving a nasty e-mail from a family member, can make you feel depleted for days.

If the kind of emotion we associate with sadness can be a drain, one of the surprising things that grieving people discover is how much of a drain "nice" emotion can also be. People are always doing kind things for someone in grief, and expressing sentiments that are beautiful and meaningful and dear. While this is all very lovely, it can be a massive drain on your emotional resources too.

The thoughtful person who drops off a cake nonetheless drains your emotion. Her kindness touches you—that drains. You try hard to show appreciation—that drains. You have to hold up your end of the small talk—that drains. And after she leaves, when you walk into the kitchen, it looks like you're holding a bake sale because of the three earlier kindly cake providers. You feel bad about how unappreciative you are of all these nice people, and that drains too.

Another huge leak in your energy tank comes from having to—for weeks and months on end—break the news of your loved one's death to people who are just getting around to hearing about it. For these people, it will be like the death just happened. Sometimes it's people you know, sometimes it's people you don't know, who may not have known your loved one all that well. But this won't prevent them from having a strong reaction to the news, and you'll have to react to their reaction. And that won't be easy. The fellow from the hardware store who delivers the propane for the barbecue grill three times a year will come to the house and ask for your husband. You'll tell him what happened and he'll be upset and tell you what a great talk he and your husband had about fishing once, and before you know it you're consoling the propane guy whose name you don't even know.

These situations deplete your energy because you probably start your day with an already low charge, having not slept well.

The perverse gods of insomnia have no more hospitable terrain than the mind of a grieving person. The unconscious mind
of someone in grief keeps nudging the conscious mind to stay
awake. It's afraid to let go of control. Somewhere, deep down,
the grieving mind knows that to rest is to loosen one's grip. To
rest is to consent to change, to relinquish the driver's seat of the
conscious mind. Particularly in the early days after a death, a
mind overtaken by grief feels that if it doesn't remain watch-
ful, another bad thing might come along and blindside it. So
your brain keeps you awake, remaining vigilant, holding on.
Insomnia reigns. And for a grieving person this can be agony,
because:

> When you have insomnia you're never really awake and
> you're never really asleep. With insomnia, nothing's real,
> everything is far away. Everything's a copy of a copy.

These lines articulate the problem perfectly. And since they're
from the film *Fight Club*, just watch the movie to see what
insomnia can lead to. There's a reason why sleep deprivation is
used as a torture technique.

If you do not have all-out insomnia, you may get some sleep,
but you may spend much of it in a kind of mental grey area,
just on the edge of consciousness where upsetting thoughts and
horrible images so pester your sleep that you are relieved to
wake up, preferring the upsetting reality of being awake to the
tormenting surrealism of poor sleep. This kind of sleep is certainly not rest.

In the wise words of W. C. Fields, "the best cure for insomnia
is to get a lot of sleep." To accomplish that, though, you may
need help. But again, the "you must" voice influences many
people. One of the more interesting taboos we encountered was
the reluctance of many grievers to use something to help them
sleep, be it a little liquor or a prescribed sleep aid.

In a country that is so overmedicated we can get Prozac for our pets, an anguished grieving person who has never demonstrated addictive behavior shouldn't hesitate to take a mild sleeping pill. If you give half a Sominex to your seventy-year-old father who's never done a drug in his life, chances are he's not going to end up on the bathroom floor singing Judy Garland songs. But a helpful New Age relative is often on hand to say, "Instead of taking a sleeping pill, why don't you have some chamomile tea?" Which is pretty much like saying, "Instead of having a sandwich, why not lick some stamps?"

If you are grieving, you don't need the chamomile tea relative or the cake-bearing neighbor. You need things that steer you toward rest. The comedian Alan King told a story about an elderly woman whose neighbors were visiting after her husband died. As they left, the neighbors promised to pray for her. The old lady replied, "I'll say my own prayers, but how about washing some dishes?"

She had a good point. In expressing care, help is so much better than words. If tomorrow morning you had to get up early and drive two hours in the snow to pick up a package, what would you rather find on the kitchen table in the morning, a "Hang in there!" card from a friend saying how bad they feel that you have to pick up the package, or *the package*, with a note saying, "Went and got this for you. Go back to bed." If only more people would get the package, not the card.

If you're sending a gift (or if you get one for yourself, which is not a bad idea), look for comforting things: bath salts, a candle, a book, a CD, a blanket (what a wonderful gift). Or there is always the greatest device for relaxation since the invention of the chair—a jigsaw puzzle. It fills the mind with abstract shapes as opposed to ideas; it may be done alone or while chatting with others; there's no electricity humming through it; and the piecing together of fragments is not a bad metaphor for the new life of a grieving person.

You need an environment that encourages rest. Someone else's mere presence may be enough to do this. One of the great obstacles to rest that grieving people face is feeling lonely, or at least uncomfortable about being alone. C. S. Lewis captures the paradox grievers feel about solitude versus company when he writes: "I want others to be about me. I dread the moments when the house is empty. If only they would talk to one another and not to me."

Much as you may yearn to rest, you'll feel uneasy when you are completely alone. As soon as the mind clears a place of tranquil solitude, the bad mental movies begin and all hope of rest is dashed.

You need to look for situations in which you can be alone but not lonely. Cafés can be a salvation. The writer Noel Riley Fitch said, "Cafés are for people who want to be alone but need company for it." Other places where people congregate but won't pester you are just as good: a park or the food court of a mall. If one happens to be near you, a campus or college environment can be a great place to hang. There's the bustle of youth, a sense of fun, and lots of people who are willfully, but *wonderfully*, clueless about the way life can pack a wallop.

Best of all is to have someone with whom you can spend time but still remain in a place of inner ease, a situation in which you don't have to talk or do, but just *be*. It's not an easy thing to come by, this special thing that the poet Rilke describes as

> The love that consists in this:
> that two solitudes
> protect
> and border
> and greet each other.

A woman who lost her child had a friend who used to let her take late-afternoon naps on the couch in the friend's den. There the grieving mother could nod off to the ambient activity of her friend getting dinner ready: spoons being tapped on bowls, pots pinging, and the eventual smell of cooking. It was an easy way to rest, "alone" but not alone. Now that's a good gift.

SPORTS

There are few sure-fire consolations, but for many people sports come about as close as you can get. When all else fails, the sick, the dying, the grief-stricken who watch sports can still get sucked into a nail-biter ninth inning, a fierce fourth quarter, a photo finish. They might even let out a cheer.

This makes sense when you consider that sports are not just games but a nexus of all kinds of human connections. People root for the college they went to, or the team from their hometown, or state, or country. A group of friends will always meet at the same bar to watch the game. People join fantasy leagues. Someone throws an amazing Super Bowl party every year. Offices start pools during March Madness, and everyone fills out brackets. There's always the friend or family member you can't wait to call when your team beats his. All these connections are renewed, on cue, as soon as the game starts" Strangers high-five, crowds suddenly scream as one, there's joy in Mudville.

Then of course there's the food that comes with the territory. It's willfully bad for you and highly enjoyable. Is there anything more colorful and consoling than a sports bar menu? How bad can life be when a bar owner thinks to cross a burrito with Buffalo wings and call it a Buffalito? Truth be told, it's not easy to maintain the image of a somber, grieving person when you have a barbecue-sauce mustache.

Even if you aren't a "sports person," it can be consoling to be in a gathering of people who are. So long as you're able to figure out "Do we like the guys in red or in white?" it's easy to get swept up in it. This happens frequently with the Olympics. Not many people know the finer points of the pommel horse, but once you get the hang of the rules and choose your team it's easy to get lost in the competition. "The Romanian judge only gave him an 8.5?! Is he nuts!"

If you can, or have the interest, *playing* sports can be an even better balm than watching them. The simplest of sports require deep focus and concentration. If you've ever seen the local senior women's bowling league, you know they are completely immersed in what they're doing; their minds couldn't possibly be anywhere else. But that's the point. Focused minds don't allow in other thoughts, and that can be a pleasant relief if you're grieving.

Playing a sport provides its own rewarding pressures as well. You set goals for yourself and see improvement bit by bit. The work and practice you put in is part of what's enjoyable. There's an inherent drive to get better, even if it means going from "I'm terrible at tennis" to "I'm still pretty bad at tennis, but at least I'm not terrible." Your skill level doesn't matter; these incremental rewards become the reason to play.

Richard Nixon said that after he left the White House in disgrace and despair what saved him was, of all things, golf. If you've ever seen a picture of Nixon on the course, it only takes a glance to see that he was no Arnold Palmer. Still, his lackluster swing was enough to get him through an international humiliation. Again, it's not your ability at a given sport; it's that it absorbs you.

If you're only a spectator, no sport does that better than baseball. Maybe it's the history, or the intrinsic Americana, or the sound of bat against ball, or maybe it's just the grass. But there's something about baseball. Toward the end of 2001, two teams in New York learned what baseball could do to console a grieving city.

On September 18, 2001, the Yankees played their first game after regular-season play resumed in the wake of the 9/11 attacks. The team was in Chicago, away from home, and seeing little point in it all. As the game was about to start, center fielder Bernie Williams recalls, "I didn't see the sense of it." Yankee manager Joe Torre echoed the feeling. He said, "Baseball was the furthest thing from our minds."

But then they took the field.

The roar for New York was deafening. Almost a thousand miles from Yankee Stadium, the Yankees saw that there was much more to what they were doing than simply playing a game. They had not only a city but a whole country that needed something to cheer for. Before the game, chants of "U-S-A!" filled the stadium as firefighters and police officers from New York were introduced and lined the field. The sentiments of Williams and Torre quickly reversed. Williams said, "It started making sense when I saw the faces of people who had lost loved ones, people who needed something to take them away for a few minutes." Torre added, "We weren't asking them to forget it; we just tried to give them a few hours of enjoyment."

Torre is right. The consolation of sports isn't about forgetting what's going on, it's about giving yourself a break, even a short one. New York City mayor Rudy Giuliani said of that time, "The only two things that got my mind off it for any period of time in the fall of 2001 were baseball and my son's football games."

A few days after the Yankees played in Chicago, the New York Mets played the first major sporting event to be held in New York City following 9/11. The game began with a tribute to those lost in the attacks, appearances by several members of the police and fire departments, and Liza Minnelli singing "New York, New York." The real moment of consolation, however, came in the eighth inning when Mets catcher Mike Piazza hit a two-run homer that lifted his team into the lead and on to an eventual victory.

Mets manager Bobby Valentine remembers, "With the crack of the bat, people stopped mourning and spontaneously stood and cheered." Sportswriter John Anderson wrote, "There's no telling how far Piazza's home run flew . . . because how do you measure the healing power of a swing . . . how do you quantify what sports truly mean to a society?" Anderson went on to credit Piazza's home run with giving the 41,000 people in attendance, as well as the millions of New Yorkers watching on TV, "A moment, maybe a fraction of a second, maybe a full minute, of pure, mindless joy."

Sports may seem trivial to some and perhaps the farthest thing from everyone's mind in a time of sadness. But when the mind is troubled, what's wrong with getting far from it? Even for just a game, an inning, or the time it takes a home run to fly out of Shea Stadium. As one reporter described Piazza's homer that night in September 2001: "It just kept going. Soaring off into the New York night. A baseball carrying an entire city's emotional baggage."

NATURE

Grandparents are one of the most consoling aspects of nature. Not only do many of them have a comforting presence, they also provide some of our gentlest lessons in what it means to age and die and be a part of the mystery of nature. Best of all, they teach these lessons in a whimsical way—a spoonful of sugar that helps the medicine of death's harsh reality go down easier.

The first death most people confront is that of a grandparent. Even before that, throughout our life with them, grandparents show us what it means to quietly shut down. Children sit on their bald grandfather's lap and ask, "Why don't you have any hair?" or "How come your face is all wrinkled?" They tug on loose skin hanging from their grandmother's arms and neck, trace the large, blue veins on her hand with a tiny fingertip. Knowingly or unknowingly, we grow up watching our grandparents die.

And when they do finally go, their passing is kinder to the system, easier to digest. First, it is more often than not a gentle death, relatively predictable and sometimes wholly expected. There's no senseless sting of tragedy, nothing that resembles a mistake or an unnatural occurrence. Grandparents tend to go peacefully, affairs in order, and with a chance for the intimations of good-bye.

For a grandchild, the experience of burying a grandparent can soften the punch of future griefs, or at least make them feel less terrifying and more like a part of life. Young, still malleable minds can assume that since grandpa is going through it, it must all be natural, normal, okay.

It's sheer circumstance of age that selects grandparents as our first teachers in grief—they happen to be the oldest people we know. But perhaps this circumstance is part of a universal design, something larger, something ancient having to do with roles within the family. Gradually, whether we realize it or not, grandparents teach us to let go forever, all the while letting us win at gin rummy and pulling quarters from behind our ears.

All other manifestations of nature's consolations do in a concentrated manner what grandparents do for us incrementally. Nature consoles not only by showing us its beauty but by making us feel there is ancient wisdom hidden in her design.

A grieving person needs to be retaught that nature is a good thing—even though it involves loss of life. One look at most books about grief shows how drawn grieving people are to a reconnection with nature. Go on Amazon, type in the word "grief," peruse the thumbnail images of the books that pop up, and you'll see a series of trees, leaves, meadows, flowers, lawns, forests, and glades—all sprinkled with dew. Grief really brings out the foliage in people!

Nature is a way for you to restore yourself after enduring the intimidating aspects of "civilization" provoked by grief. You find yourself stuck in many situations that are uncomfortably unnatural. If you've kept a vigil at the bedside of someone suffering a long illness, you've been surrounded by the nightmare gadgetry of a hospital—tubes and charts and monitors and other machines. If the loved one has died suddenly, you have been in a world of official protocols and portentous phone calls. Or, at the very least, you have inhabited the land of funerals and funeral planning, a realm that can make you feel that a score of somber organ music has played under your life for days on end.

After living with the unfamiliar abstractions of grief, you can see why finally getting your hands dirty in the garden again can be a consoling way to come, literally, back down to earth. There's a reason we use the term "down to earth" to describe people who are genuine and easy to be around. In a time of grief, people look for the activities, the people, and the circumstances that let them kick off their funereal dress shoes.

Another way nature consoles is by restoring you to an anonymity you rarely have during grief. Grief makes you stand out. You get attention, you're thought to be "special." You get thrown, unwillingly, to the center of the universe. In walks the widow, and every head turns and tilts sweetly—the way people look at a puppy. You are a minor celebrity. Friends and family come from all over to see you, worry about you, think about you, and keep asking you how you're doing. It's all very thoughtful on their part, but being at the center of the universe is exhausting and stressful.

After spending time in the outsized world of tragedy, people long to be restored to their customary scale, to be a self, a human being, a body, and not the leading man or lady of a major drama. In Mel Brooks's famous sketch "The 2000-Year-Old Man," the eponymous character is asked by an interviewer if people back then had some sort of "higher power" they believed in. He replies:

> Yes, we had a deity. A guy named Phil. He was a very big guy. And scary, 'cause he could just crush you. So we'd pray to him. We'd pray: "O Phil. . . . Please don't hurt us." But then, one day, a lightning bolt came and BAM! it struck Phil. So we all looked around and said to each other: "There's something bigger than Phil."

Nature reminds us that there's "something bigger than Phil." And something bigger than us. In so doing it consoles by undercutting the "grief hype."

Nature pays no attention to you, or your grief, or your life. Nature doesn't try to help, or say the right thing, or give you what it thinks you need. Nature is unaware, unconcerned. You are rendered "small" in comparison to nature and all its awesome manifestations. And you don't have to be at the Grand Canyon to have this feeling; a pelting rainstorm will do the trick. Even though experiencing nature reminds us of our rather insignificant role in the larger momentum of life, it does so in a way that feels comfortingly real and therefore calming. It reminds us that we are not in charge—and that's a good thing, a burden lifted.

At its best, nature also reminds us how good it is—how right and fine and bracing a phenomenon it can be. In just about any form nature makes us feel this way. We get this feeling even from instances of nature that are so familiar we forget they are, indeed, nature—things like kids and pets.

You can luxuriate in crying alone with a pet. A good ten minutes of sobs intensified by your dog's soulful, upturned eyes can be quite healthy. Being around young children is another familiar instance of nature that can be just as good, but for the opposite reason: you don't allow yourself to cry in front of them. You want to be "up" and doing, and letting them bop you on the head with a Nerf bat.

When you are exposed to nature, whether in these small, everyday instances or in its grander and more breathtaking forms, you can come away with the feeling that nature is an innately correct design, even if it includes death. An inability to accept nature is a kind of neurosis. In fact, a good layperson's definition of neurosis might be "fear of nature"—one's own as well as the outdoors. To open yourself up to nature is to welcome "the real" in all its aspects, which is perhaps why we use the words "real" and "natural" in interchangeable ways. Nature makes people more real.

And so does grief.

So much of our normal life is an amped up escape from the real. One of the few "gifts" of grief is that it damn sure returns people to reality. There's nothing more real than someone you love being dead. With just about anything else you can lie to yourself—who you are, whether or not people love you, what the future may hold. These things we can finesse. But not grief. The loved one is gone forever, and that's that.

But while grief is the dark side of reality, nature is the brighter side of it. Being exposed to it, in whatever form, gives us a sense that something wise and benign is behind all of it. In Shakespeare's play *As You Like It*, an exiled duke lives in the forest. The downside of his life is his exile, the upside is what his exposure to nature has given him. He rhapsodizes about his woodsy surroundings:

> This our life, exempt from public haunt,
> Finds tongues in trees, books in running brooks,
> Sermons in stones, and good in everything.

The duke believes that "sweet are the uses of adversity." It is one of Shakespeare's best "unfamous" lines. He's saying that without the adversity that exiled the duke from public life, he would never have been able to hear the sermons of the stones. While there is very little that is sweet about the adversity of grief, nature helps us realize not that grief is a good thing, but that life is.

INDULGENCE

The journalist David Rieff wrote a book about losing his mother, the writer Susan Sontag, to leukemia. The book has an eyebrow-raising, blunt title. It's called *Swimming in a Sea of Death*, which is clearly meant to describe how those hard final days of his mother's life felt to him. For many people, the loss of a loved one comes after being so steeped in illness or tragedy that it feels as if death itself has soaked into the survivor's house, her room, her clothes, her hair, her body and soul. Many grieving people have indeed been in a sea of death from which they now look to be rescued.

For some who grieve, a book about *their* experience of having someone die could just as easily be called *Swimming in a Sea of Self-Denial.* Grieving people have often been through a long period of having to put their needs second to the needs of the dying person. In fighting the good fight, people forgo showers, sleep in contorted positions on hospital chairs, maintain arduous vigils. This is a right and natural thing to do for someone you love. And because most of us feel, as Reiff phrased it, that "the dying have right of way," it's a given that their needs are placed before our own, that our small discomforts can't be compared with their suffering.

But self-denial takes a toll. In the words of William Butler Yeats, "Too long a sacrifice can make a stone of the heart." Unrelenting self-denial can dull your life force and make you feel that *your* needs are of little value in the scheme of things. If you have swum through a particularly difficult sea of death, you may find certain urges rising after your loved one is gone. You may begin to cry out for life rather than death, to yearn for the opposite of self-denial—which, frankly, is a little self-indulgence.

While it may be indelicate to say so, indulgence can be very consoling!

One of the common ways grieving people console themselves is by indulging in food. In her essay "S Is for Sad," the food writer M. F. K. Fisher describes "the mysterious appetite that often surges in us when our hearts are about to break and our lives seem bleakly empty." A man Fisher knew, whom she describes as "well raised," showed up at her house one day "in a state of shock" at something he had done the night his much-loved wife died. Having watched her fade away "for two nights and a day," the evening after her death the man drove up the California coast to see Fisher. Along the way, Fisher says:

> he must have stopped at four or five big restaurants and eaten a thick steak at each one, with other things he usually ignored, like piles of French-fried potatoes, slabs of pie, and whatever bread was in front of him. . . He drank cup after cup of searing black coffee, with or without food, in a dozen little joints along the road, and then left them humming and whistling.

By the time he got to Fisher's house he couldn't believe what he had done, how he had indulged himself. He said to her,

"How could I? How could I?—and she not yet in her coffin?" He felt like a heel. But Fisher defended his inclinations and understood them as an attempt to take in some hedonistic "life" after all that somber death. As she phrased it, "The truth is that most bereaved souls crave nourishment more tangible than prayers; they want a steak. What is more they need a steak. Preferably they need it rare. . ."

Another area of life in which some grieving people like to indulge is sex. This itch for indulgence manifests itself in feelings and odd urges without your necessarily acting upon those urges. But sometimes that happens too.

The former poet laureate Donald Hall chronicled his brushes with indulgence after the death of his wife Jane Kenyon. Hall and Kenyon had had a wonderful marriage. It was portrayed in an Emmy-winning documentary entitled *A Life Together,* and many of the poems Hall wrote in the last years of Kenyon's life were love poems about his wife. They had been married for twenty-three years when she died on April 22, 1995.

Two weeks later Hall bought condoms.

He began to look for, and to find, sex. He wrote in the third person about this surprising lust. "His immediate grief confused him into feeling alive," he writes in one poem. Such a touching line. This pathetic, unfettered appetite. Like the man in Fisher's story, he must have said, "How could I? How could I?—and she not yet in her coffin?" But as Fisher explains it, this urge is not only normal but essentially admirable. She claims that, "Like every other physical phenomenon, there is always good reason for this hunger if we are blunt enough to recognize it." Those people she calls "the prettifiers of human passion," though, won't admit it. She says, "It's as if our bodies, wiser than we who wear them, call out for encouragement and strength, and in spite of the patterns of proper behavior we have learned, compel us to answer, and to eat."

To eat, to lust, to love, to indulge. It's an instinct of soul as much as body. We can see this instinct in our most sacred symbolisms, this primal urge to exorcise death with new life, this urge to transform the cross of Good Friday into the egg of Easter Sunday. (In many mythologies the egg is a symbol of both food and procreation, the ideal metaphor for a life force.) We can see it in something as basic as the compulsion people have to show up at the home of the bereaved with food. Food is life and an acceptable sublimation of this natural urge. (You can't exactly show up at shivah and say, "So sorry for your loss. How about a quick roll in the hay?")

Sex, though just as common an urge for some grieving people as food is for others, is not as easy to talk about. Sex has far more shame attached to it than food, so it can be harder to process. A second dessert can be forgiven; asking the waitress if she wants to go home with you is harder to brush off. One woman spoke with us about the time after she lost her fiancé, very young. She described her uncharacteristic behavior using what she herself called an uncharacteristic word: "For the first and only time in my life, I went wild and fucked like a bunny." She was clearly embarrassed by her language, so it was not easy to imagine this dignified lady doing what she said.

Sex may have a stigma, but the inclination toward sex comes from the same place as the drive for food: a desire for life, a need to feel the life force palpably and physically. In Tennessee Williams's play *A Streetcar Named Desire*, the character Blanche DuBois has fled her life in Mississippi to live with her sister Stella in New Orleans. It turns out that Blanche has left her former life after earning a reputation as the town trollop, even having an affair with one of her high-school-age students. But as Blanche explains, she did these things to fill herself with life. In a house where her father, mother, and sister all died, she says, "the Grim Reaper had put up his tent on our doorstep." "Desire," she explains, "is the opposite of death."

If that's true, it makes sense that this desire to have some reconnection with a life force, whether through sex or another form of indulgence, is felt by a dying person just as much as by someone in grief. In their last bit of time, dying people often become interested in, even fixated on, doing things that remind them that *today* they are alive, regardless of what the case may be tomorrow. In her book *Final Exam,* Pauline Chen tells the true story of an older man with a terminal illness. As it became clear that he wouldn't be around much longer, he insisted on taking his wife shopping for a tuxedo at the finest store in Beverly Hills. She said he must have tried on dozens of them.

> I have no idea why he did that. It was just crazy. We had no functions to attend, and deep down I knew he would never wear it. But I kept quiet and went along and watched him try on every tuxedo and buy the most expensive one. It was as if he needed to reassure himself that he was alive. Maybe, just for a few minutes, he wanted to believe he was not going to die.

If you are caring for someone who is dying or helping someone through grief, it's important to recognize as normal this will to feel apart from death. Give the person some slack. There's nothing wrong with letting your loved one indulge. Most cases are mild.

If you are grieving, know that what feels like "bad behavior" or "inappropriate thoughts" are really rooted in a retroactive rage against what Dylan Thomas famously called "the dying of the light." You are indulging as a way to let yourself know that "in my hour of darkness there is still a light that shines on me." It may be best to heed the advice of that song and let it be.

SOLIDARITY

Almost immediately upon the death of a mutual loved one, people feel the need to share a common space with others. They gather. And at the larger of these gatherings, people receive some sort of physical iconography that will help them stay connected after they leave—a T-shirt, a candle, a flower, a ribbon, an armband, a flyer, a Mass card.

This deep need for connection with others can bring out creativity and cleverness in people. They find interesting ways to express solidarity, from the now common practice of commemorative tattoos to memorial websites to even more innovative gestures we have heard or read about.

A family from California was vacationing in Italy when their seven-year-old son, Nicholas, was killed after being shot in a botched robbery. The devastated family made the decision to donate their son's organs to seven severely ill Italian citizens, some of whom were young teenagers. Nicholas's father said, after word got out about this, "Individual gestures of solidarity sprang up immediately and have never ceased." He went on to describe one of the more unique tributes:

> For years, a school in Sicily has had two clocks in its entrance hall, one showing the time in Italy, the other in California, so that students will feel the connection every day. Italians of all ages feel so close to him that they refer to him not by his full name but as "piccolo Nicholas," little Nicholas.

These meaningful shows of support are one version of solidarity. Another version, which can be just as valid, is solidarity that is fun. For Americans, fun is not only a legitimate form of solidarity but the preferred one. A popular video called "Pink Glove Dance" can be seen online. It was made for breast cancer awareness and support. In it the employees of a suburban medical center all wear pink surgical gloves and dance throughout the hospital to the song "Down" by Jay Sean, which has lyrics like, "Baby don't worry. You are my only. You won't be lonely, even if the sky is falling." In making the video, everyone got involved, from surgeons to janitors, cafeteria workers, and patients. If you have to explain to someone what's best about Americans, this video might be a good place to start. Exhibitions of solidarity that bind us to one another but also unleash joy are our way of offering support: music videos, dances, barbecues, T-shirts, sports tournaments, funny bumper stickers—you name it, we come up with it.

Underneath our inclination to display solidarity is a basic human truth: *We get our sense of security from others.* This is true not only in a time of crisis but throughout our lives. The mere presence of another human being is, in a way, all we need to feel consoled. It doesn't even matter who that person is, just he or she *being there* provides solidarity. How many airline passengers have spent the first half of their flight vying for control of the armrest with the stranger next to them—then, feel compelled to clutch that same stranger when the plane encounters turbulence? In all sorts of "turbulence" we want another human being to reach for. It needn't matter if they can help us, their presence alone will suffice. If, for example, you watch a scary movie on a rainy night in a house all alone, it is far more terrifying than if you watch that same scary movie on that same rainy night in a house with a seven-year-old child. The kid certainly won't save you from Hannibal Lecter, but that small presence is enough to help you feel protected.

This basic human need for solidarity undergirds our self-definition and shapes our daily lives. We get our sense of security from belonging to, and feeling "safe" within, certain emotional affiliations. It's as if every one of us has a series of concentric circles around us, with each circle a kind of fort in which we feel safe. You could call these "Circles of Solidarity," and there are five basic ones. There is one's *mate*, a spouse or partner. There is *family*, both the family you create and the one you were born into (which are sometimes intertwined but often distinct entities). There are *friends,* and for many this circle can be even stronger than *family*. There are *groups,* collectives based on proximity or common purpose such as neighborhood, workplace, school, and all sorts of activities that create commonality. (We heard about a funeral in which the man who died was a soccer referee. The church was packed with soccer referees—dressed as soccer referees! *That's* a group.) Finally there is *nation*, which at times is a mere abstraction but may be reinvigorated by events.

Mate, family, friends, groups, nation: these circles make us who we are. In a tragedy, one of these enclosures gets breached, so people flee to another circle for safety. A spouse dies, the *mate* circle cracks, and the widow begins to get more involved in her church group than ever before, thereby shoring up the *group* circle. A high schooler has a friend die at school, and rather than hang around with peers as one would expect, he wants to spend more time around the house, enveloped in the stronger fort of *family* for a while. The *group* circle doesn't feel strong enough to the teen; he may cry on the shoulders of friends, but he needs the more solid shoulders of his parents.

People in grief may have no desire to leave their main circle, and may do so only if they sense the circle isn't solid anymore. When tested by tragedy, the usual dynamics of a circle matter less than its solidity.

There is, for example, a common belief that if a couple experiences the death of a child, their marriage is destined for divorce. This is talked about so much that couples who lose a child almost begin looking at each other and thinking, "Well, hon, clock's ticking, better start breaking up." But it turns out that this assumption may not be as accurate as people think.

There is, in fact, no conclusive evidence that couples who lose a child are more likely to divorce. According to the support group Compassionate Friends, a nationwide network of local support groups for grieving parents, many couples see the *mate* circle grow stronger during a mutual grief. This conclusion may be biased because it's based only on the experience of members of a support group. But even that is telling. It says that couples who are willing to go to a support group and talk and be compassionate and think of each other as friends have a much better chance to weather the harrowing task of burying a child.

Marriages that do end under these circumstances may have had problems to begin with. Grief can be a magnifying glass over a relationship, enlarging its problems. A death may be used as a sort of "get-out-of-jail-free card" to end things. In the film *Adaptation,* Meryl Streep plays Susan Orlean, a journalist in an unhappy marriage. Susan has begun falling for a horticulturist, John, whom she is writing a story about. During one of their interviews he tells her how his wife left him after her parents were killed in a car accident. Susan replies, "If that happened to me, I'd probably leave my husband too." "Why?" John asks, and Susan answers, "Because I could. Because no one would judge me." While some people do take this way out, the truth remains that marriages don't usually end *because* of grief. Grief only expedites a process that may already have been under way.

As some circles become more solid during grief, entirely new circles emerge as well. After losing her only son, Sissy Spacek's character in *In the Bedroom* struggles with how little solidarity she feels with her husband. She eventually speaks to a priest who tells her a story about another woman who also lost a child. The other woman had a dream in which she saw, "encircling the earth, an endless line of mothers." She also saw herself in the line. At one point "the line divided," and she realized why. She "knew that all the millions of women on her side were the mothers who lost children." Upon finishing the story, the priest adds, "She seemed to find great comfort in that." The *family* circle may have been broken, but the new circle of "mothers who've lost children" provides some consolation.

Historically the most common version of this tendency to reestablish circles of solidarity occurs when one's nation comes under attack. When this happens, the threat feels so grave that *all* the other circles become more important. One of the reasons why those walls of pictures that were posted in lower Manhattan in the weeks after 9/11 were so deeply moving, beyond the obvious reasons, is that they so vividly encapsulated all the circles of solidarity people have in their lives. As the playwright John Guare (an avid New Yorker who lives in lower Manhattan) observed, "Every person in every one of those pictures was looking at someone they loved." A spouse, a son, a best friend, someone from the office party at work, or a pal from the bowling team—all the circles represented.

In a time of grief, it's important to recognize that your basic need for the security of a group is more important than the need for "displays" of group triumphalism. It's not uncommon for people to become so determined to have a "show" of solidarity that they undermine the kind of solidarity you really want.

Here's an example. Two students from the film department of a small university were killed in a car accident while returning to school after a long weekend. Knowing that this would be a brutal experience for members of the college, the dean allowed the film building to remain open, around the clock, for forty-eight hours, and made sure the place was continuously supplied with food so that students could gather and be together. People began showing up all day. One student then proposed organizing a candlelight procession that would encircle the entire perimeter of the university. He was so determined to have this (albeit well-meaning) *show* of campus solidarity that he kept turning up at the film building with massive boxes of candles and flyers about "the event." The students, however, were much more content to be together in the way they were. By nightfall people had begun to bring pillows and blankets into the lobby of the building, and other kids curled up in corners with their laptops doing homework while others just sat and talked. Faculty and staff members stayed around until the wee hours too—talking, eating, just being there. It was a warm environment of true solidarity. "Procession Guy" nonetheless continued to lobby for his event until people were about to throttle him. He finally got the message, and the students remained together in a warm, close atmosphere of authentic solidarity.

But this guy's misreading of the situation cuts to the heart of the issue of solidarity as a consolation for the grieving. It is much more about *physical* safety and comfort than people realize.

While solidarity may manifest itself in the kinds of demonstrations this student was trying to drum up, underneath it all is a very basic desire for a sense of shelter. Emily Dickinson once signed off a letter, "I felt it shelter to speak to you." That's how it feels to be around certain people: you feel safe. In times of grief, this need for emotional shelter intensifies. Tragedy and grief will make you feel terribly exposed. Exiled from a once immutable circle, you are now out in the elements with no protection. e. e. cummings once wrote, "My love is building a building around you." This is what grieving people want. Protection, safety, a building—not a parade.

A recent *Los Angeles Times* article reported on a study at the University of Toronto that showed a connection between loneliness and feelings of coldness. The article, entitled "Cold and Lonely Go Together—Literally," described a test in which some people were asked to think about a time when they felt socially isolated while others were asked to concentrate on a time when

they felt socially accepted. Both groups were then asked to esti-
mate the temperature of the room. On average, people assigned
to ruminate about rejection said seventy-one degrees—about
five degrees cooler than the second group.

In another experiment, people played a ball-tossing game
in which some of the players would receive the ball only twice.
Afterward they were asked to rate their desire for hot coffee, hot
soup, or an icy Coke. The people who were all but ignored during the game showed "a greater preference for hot liquids than
those who were not." Grief makes people feel cold.

The poet Karen Swenson, on the death of her father,
writes:

> The wind comes in my window like
> the breath of silence where my father spoke.
> It is as if the opening of the earth for him
> has left some door ajar
> and I,
> in this vast room of fields,
> am shivering in its draft.

That grief can make people feel cold is something that people
innately understand. For example, all the food that people bring
to those in grief is hot and thick comfort food, the culinary version of a blanket. Soups, stews, and casseroles—these are the
kinds of food our intuition tells us are right to give someone in
grief. No one says, "So sorry to hear about your loss. I made you
some prosciutto and melon." We seem to know that for a grieving person to feel comfortable, they must be within something
solid, even if that something is food. The word "comfort" has
nothing to do with cozy and soft. It comes from the root word
"fortis" meaning "strong," as in "fort." Being comfortable means
feeling safe, like being in a fort.

Some people, when faced with the worst life has to offer, are still able to exercise an innate wisdom about what comfort truly is, and that understanding leads them toward consolation, even from inside the belly of the beast. We heard of a family with three boys, the youngest of whom died from an accidental drug overdose. He hadn't come home the night before, and the worried family was making calls and scouring the town to find him. The middle brother was at college a hundred miles from where the family lived, and was on the phone with his frantic mother who was at home with the father. During this call the father got a call from the oldest brother who was out searching the town.

So all four of them were connected through two phone lines. Suddenly the oldest brother said, "Wait, I think I see his car," and began running toward it. He looked in the window to find his missing brother in the front seat—face blue, clearly dead. One can only imagine what happened over those two phone lines.

The son at college drove two hours to his family's house. Later, when he recounted the story of returning home, he said the first thing he noticed when he walked in the house was a fire in the fireplace. Someone with great emotional intelligence (a family member? a friend of the family? a neighbor?) had lit a fire, which was warmly crackling when he came through the door—as good an example of comfort as one could find.

Later that night, after everyone had left, this family of four, which a day earlier had been a family of five, was finally alone. One of the brothers went into the parents' room where both of them were lying on the bed talking. The boy joined them, actually climbing up on the bed with them. After a while the other brother came in and also lay down with them. Both these boys would not normally do something like this, but one brother said, "It just felt right at the time." So the four of them lay there together for hours, talking and crying in solidarity, building a building around each other.

CYNICISM

Dorothy Parker, writer and notorious wit, used to answer her phone, "What fresh hell is this?"

While this is not the sort of salutation most people would use, if you have suffered through an illness, death, or grief, you know the feeling. Each day can bring some new wrinkle of awfulness you hadn't counted on. Even when the news is good for a grieving person, it often has a bad flip side.

A girl who recently lost her father told us about opening her acceptance letter to the college she dreamed of attending. It was a moment of joy and victory whoops. But the celebration soon faded into a flood of sadness as the girl realized that her father, who six months earlier had been at the kitchen table helping her with the application, would never know he has a daughter at the University of Pennsylvania.

"Robbed" is a word people use a lot around grief. They not only feel robbed by all those days of suffering in hospitals; they also feel robbed of the ability to experience the good days they should be having. And these daily robberies make people mad.

Mad as hell.

The dirty little secret of grief is rage. While most laypeople think the main emotion a grieving person needs to purge is sadness, psychiatric professionals seem to talk much more about rage.

Elizabeth Kubler-Ross was a groundbreaking psychiatrist who worked with terminally ill patients and their families. She was the first person to codify what she called the Five Stages of Grief, one of which is Anger. (The others are Denial, Depression, Bargaining, and Acceptance.) If you look at old photographs of Kubler-Ross with her patients, you'll notice some of them have a small length of rubber hose with them. Old patients, young patients, male patients, female patients—they're all carrying these hoses. Kubler-Ross explains that this odd piece of psychological equipment has to do with the rage that comes with grief.

> We use a rubber hose because, first of all, it is inexpensive, is easily available, and can be tucked in any bag, can be used in any place. It also reinforces the power in our arms when we feel like striking or hitting someone in rage and anger. If no rubber hose is available, it is very easy to take a bath towel and fold it, or, if necessary, we can use our fists. But with a rubber hose the worst that can happen is that we will end up with a few blisters on our fingers. The main point, though, is that when a patient or member of the patient's family feels an incredible sense of anger or unfairness, he simply uses the rubber hose and beats a mattress or a pillow or a couch, hitting that object instead of the person toward whom the anger is directed. He can then externalize and ventilate and scream out his rage without hurting anyone.

This may seem pretty extreme, a technique left over from the 1970s when Kubler-Ross was using it. But while psychiatry may change from decade to decade, grief doesn't. It remains the cluster bomb of emotions it was 30 years ago when Kubler-Ross was writing, and 2,500 years ago when Sophocles said in *Antigone*, "Grief teaches the steadiest mind to waver." When steady minds waver, it's good for them to have a safe way to blow off steam. Who knows, if Kubler-Ross were alive today, in our angry age, those hoses might be selling like crazy on the Home Shopping Network.

If you are grieving, the most common substitute for a length of rubber hose—something you can keep hidden, ready to whip out when some fresh hell upsets you—is plain old cynicism.

One woman told us about her brother who had lost his wife a year and a half ago. The sister and brother were driving, on their way to do some shopping for the holidays, when the brother sneered, "Christmas is a lot of bullshit." It appalled this woman that her nice Catholic brother could say such a thing, and she talked about the incident as if she suddenly had Pontius Pilate in the passenger seat of her SUV.

But cynicism is a way of releasing rage. It not only feels good to you, it's also relatively harmless to those around you. Cynicism generalizes rage, refines it into a philosophical stance. Rather than make a direct attack on someone, you can take your rage and point it at an abstract target. Like Christmas.

If the brother had made a more specific comment, something like, "You know what I want for Christmas? A better sister," that sort of rage would be harmful. If he took a more specific swipe at Christmas—"I wouldn't have let them in my inn either!"— that would have been an attack on his religion. But cynicism tends to be benignly general, harmlessly vague. The person who wears a T-shirt that says "Life Sucks" isn't being very specific.

Cynicism is just a benign version of the sort of thing people do to get out their frustrations while driving. They're in the car pent up with rage about obligations, work issues, traffic, and so forth, so when another driver cuts them off, they project all their anger onto a phantom driver veiled inside the anonymity of his car. If those same people bumped into that driver as he was walking on the sidewalk, they'd say a polite "Excuse me" and let him pass. They wouldn't say, "Learn how to walk, buddy!" and give him the finger.

Like the sister with her snarky brother, we tend to be accepting of the "nice" aspects of grief but not the "mean" ones. If the same two siblings were driving and the brother said, "Sis, I get really sad around Christmas because I miss my wife, and I think

I need to cry," the sister would have said, "Go ahead, cry!" She would have pulled over the car and let him bawl as long as he wanted, and she probably would have felt glad to be there for him. But when it comes to some of the darker manifestations of grief, people hit the taboo alarm. We prefer the inspirational to the cynical, the heartwarming to the dyspeptic. We read *Tuesdays with Morrie* and other kindly chronicles. A book called *Thursdays with Schmuck* would not be a best-seller. But you don't always need a shoulder to cry on. Sometimes you need a shoulder upon which to say grumpy things because it feels good to do so.

Alice Roosevelt Longworth, an Olympian cynic, once said the immortal words, "If you can't say anything nice about somebody, then come and sit by me." It can be invaluable to have an Alice Roosevelt as part of your personal kitchen cabinet.

Those close to a grieving person should understand the nature of this cynicism. It's not necessarily rooted in malice. It just happens to be consoling for you to sandblast with negativity some of the "positives" you feel betrayed by. In particular, hope.

Emily Dickinson wrote, "Hope is that thing with feathers that perches in the soul," to which Woody Allen once replied:

> How wrong Emily Dickinson was! Hope is not "that thing with feathers." The thing with feathers has turned out to be my nephew. I must take him to a specialist in Zurich.

You might be more inclined to accept Woody Allen's view of hope, because grief is always post-hope. Grieving means hope is gone, the miracle didn't happen, the loved one died. So why not take the cynic's view of hope? H. L. Mencken defined a cynic as "a man who, when he smells a flower, looks around for a coffin." For many people in grief, the last time they smelled a flower there *was* a coffin around.

Cynicism is the opposite of hope. Indulging in it may help you exorcise the demons of all those false hopes you let yourself be suckered into. Losing a loved one makes it feel like you've been deluding yourself to be hopeful—about a spontaneous recovery or about the rosy future you planned with someone who died. In either case you feel, as the line in "Funeral Blues" says, "I thought that love would last forever: I was wrong."

C. S. Lewis, with his wife Joy dying by inches, clung to what he refers to as "all the false hopes we had." No one would accuse Lewis of being a cynic—not the whimsical allegorist of *The Chronicles of Narnia* or the lucid theologian of his religious writings. But here's how he cynically ticks off a list of these "no show" hopes:

> Not hopes raised merely by our own wishful thinking;
> hopes encouraged, even forced upon us, by false diagnoses,
> by X-ray photographs, by strange remissions, by one
> temporary recovery that might have ranked as a miracle.
> Step by step we were "led up the garden path." Time
> after time when He seemed most gracious He was really
> preparing the next torture.

Yes, the man who wrote *Mere Christianity*, one of the most eloquent and esteemed arguments for religious belief, just referred to his God as a torturer. But, as is true of most people in like circumstances, Lewis's cynicism was only a phase. Rage is a powerful feeling but usually finite. A certain amount of frustration, once blown, will probably make you feel better. Most people soon return to their regular selves. If you find yourself enjoying a bit of cynicism, just be sure not to overdo it. Try not to let it become a permanent part of who you are. Do it only to console and heal, with the hope of weaning yourself off it once you're in better shape. As the Buddhist writer Shunryu Suzuki said, "You should not mistake medicine for food."

If it's okay for a genius like Lewis to be a cynic for a while, it's all right for mere mortals like us. So when you find yourself alone in the house, treat yourself to a spa of consoling cynicism. Say the worst possible things. Don't be afraid to say things about the loved one you lost, either. You're doing it in order to get ugly, inflated feelings out of you. It's better than holding them in.

A good time to do this is while vacuuming. The vacuum motor is roaring, so you can't hear yourself saying the things you can't believe are coming out of your mouth, and there's something about the back-and-forth wrenching motion of your arm that helps pump up the fury. You'll get out some rage and feel better—and your carpets will be clean.

NORMALCY

If someone has been physically injured and is in need of rehabilitation, it's understood that a large part of that person's progress depends on his or her attitude. People are encouraged to think positive and aim high. They are taught to feel positive not only about their goals for the future but about what they are able to do each day—to take delight in small steps. High aims are just an accumulation of "small aims," a minute-by-minute focus on each incremental accomplishment. The recovery mantra for injured people might be "Be patient" or, even better, "Think big, appreciate small."

In grief you may lack the dramatic physical evidence of someone with a physical injury—you don't have the casts or bandages or Frankensteinian stitches of the felled athlete—but whatever "part" of yourself performs the function of *being happy* has taken a hard hit and is no less injured than the ski bum's femur.

When you are trying to recover from grief, you may fail to appreciate the baby-step improvements you make, or even to recognize them. It may not seem like a big deal when you involuntarily start humming along to radio music for the first time, but it is. These first moments of even the most banal contentment should be seized on because they let you know that the ability to feel "okay" is still in you somewhere, and not gone forever. Granted, these little accomplishments won't interest others as a physical injury would, and it's doubtful that your friends will be calling each other to say, "Did you hear? Murray's humming again!" Still, initial progress, no matter how insignificant it seems, should not be sniffed at any more than someone taking their first wobbly steps down a hospital hallway after a severe injury. You can't run if you can't, first, wiggle your toe. Humming to the radio is a toe wiggle. Part of recovery is relearning how to be happy, and these small instances are the earliest signs that it's happening.

This is the consolation of what we call simple *normalcy*.

If you are grieving, the little activities, sensations, and interactions of the day, taken for granted by most of us, can be a great consolation. Often the first restorative seconds you have are when you find yourself getting lost in an everyday task. Getting back to the gym, lingering in the park to watch a few impressive skateboarders, passing along that first piece of juicy, postgrief gossip, or—something that's probably healed more people than aspirin—popcorn and a movie.

Daphne Merkin, after being stricken with a depression that almost killed her, wrote these lines about her first experience with the consolation of normalcy. They describe how she finished reading a novel at her friend's beach house:

> It was the first book to absorb me—the first I could read
> at all—since before I went to the hospital. I came to the

last page on the third afternoon of my visit. It was about 4:30, the time of day that, by mid-August, brings with it a whiff of summer's end. I looked up into the startlingly blue sky; one of the dogs was sitting at my side, her warm body against my leg, drying me off after the swim I had recently taken. I could begin to see the curve of fall up ahead. There would be new books to read, new films to see, and new restaurants to try. I envisioned myself writing again, and it didn't seem like a totally preposterous idea.

Getting back into the daily routines of our life is also helpful. The common rituals of the day give us a sense of order and a feeling of safety. They are the little "knowns" that make big "unknowns," like death and grief, more bearable. People underestimate how consoling these little "to-dos" can be.

A father was talking about losing his wife, and the mother of his eight-year-old son, to a long bout with cancer. The boy's nightly routine was always the same: the father made sure his son took a bath, was read a story, sang a song, and said a prayer before going to sleep—this had been the routine just about every night of the boy's life. The man said, "Every night he had a bath, a story, a song, and a prayer. It was just how we always did things." So on the day the boy's mother died, what did they do? The boy got a bath, a story, a song, and a prayer. The only difference was, that night the son asked if his dad would leave the door open and keep a light on in the hall.

It's easy to see how these little rituals of the day might go by the wayside in the face of tragedy or death, even an expected death. But this father was smart enough to know what a consolation basic normalcy can be.

Even at a time of high emotion, an occasional return to normalcy can break the tension. In the film *In the Bedroom*, the pent-up recriminations between the husband and wife over the death of their son come flying out in probably the ugliest argument of their lives. At the boiling point of their unforgettable and unforgivable exchange, there's a knock at the door. When the man goes to answer, standing there is a little girl selling candy for her school. He is caught off guard by the girl's simple, sweet presence and her innocent sales spiel. He hesitates a few awkward moments, then begins asking prices and fumbling for change in his pocket. He walks back into the tense house with half a dozen jumbo candy bars, which he sets on the table in front of his wife. She's caught off guard. From that point on, though, things between the couple are lighter. They talk to each other in a gentler, more humane way. The operatic aftermath of a terrible fight is cut down to size when normalcy knocks, literally, at the door.

The way that normalcy goes about its business can be refreshing for a grieving person who is weary of being treated differently by others. A man who lost his wife remembered that, a few weeks after she died, he had a call from a colleague he hadn't heard from in a while. The colleague didn't know that the man's wife had recently died, and the two men had a long chat about work, golf, and regular guy stuff. The colleague never got around to asking the obligatory "How's the family?" question, so the conversation ended without the man mentioning that his wife had died only weeks earlier. But this felt terrific to him! He was so glad to be given an oasis of normalcy in an otherwise unremitting treck of grief. Of course, if the colleague had found out that this man's wife had died, he'd probably want to jump out a window for being so insensitive. Little would he have known what a saving grace that normal, emotionless, run-of-the-mill phone call was. A grieving man was restored to being "just a guy at work." When your work identity can trump your grief identity for a while, at least from nine to five, it's a step on the road to healing.

As the frenzy of activity surrounding grief winds down, the question arises of when and how to return to work. Some people have a very strong relationship with their work. For many, it's second only to the people they love in the hierarchy of what matters—and sometimes a very close second. Work can be tremendously healing. It gets a grieving person back into the routine of functioning in the "real world." Jobs have built-in schedules, deadlines, and a sense of being useful again and not just a grieving person stuck in an unproductive groove. After a long period of being doted on in many ways, work helps restore your identity as a competent person. It helps you announce to the world, "I am once again someone who can be relied on."

But work can also set you back a bit. Viktor Frankl, the psychologist and Holocaust survivor who wrote *Man's Search for Meaning,* coined the phrase "Sunday Neurosis," which basically describes people who are so intensely dedicated to their job that the weekend depresses them. Now, almost half the people in the world could probably be said to have a mild case of Sunday Neurosis, but with grieving people it can be a major problem. They dive into their job obsessively and to the near exclusion of other activities. Work becomes a way not to reengage with the world but to lock oneself away from it, to avoid any *feeling* and to skirt the truly difficult work of healing. Be aware of this pitfall.

But for most people, work is more than just something positive, it's a salvation and one of the more helpful elements of the consolation of normalcy.

In Tony Kushner's play *Angels in America,* a man grappling with the stigma and sufferings of AIDS has a dream in which a woman appears to him. The two have a face-to-face conversation, and at one point she whispers in his ear, "Deep down there is a part of you—the innermost part—that's entirely free of disease. I can see that." This is the sort of thing normalcy does for a grieving person. It whispers into your ear that deep down there is a part of you that is not grief. In that innermost part you are still you. A normal person, grieving.

READING

> I had never really enjoyed the written word in the prior forty-two years of my life, as I could honestly say I had not even read enough books to fill the digits on one hand. Since Audrey's death, I have read close to one hundred books. I just can't seem to get enough.—Jerre Petersen, *Grief Works*

This comment, made by a man whose daughter died at age eight, is pretty typical of people in grief. It's common for them to go on reading jags. They suddenly have a ravenous, almost primal, hunger to read, especially materials related to grief. A woman told us how her husband, normally "not much of a reader," had recently begun to get the bug. She said, "Now he's always grabbing a book from my pile." It's rare to walk into the home of someone dealing with a long-term grief and not find at least a small "pile" of books on the subject.

In the early days and weeks of grief, you may find that reading *anything* is a challenge. The microwaving instructions on a frozen dinner require too much concentration. You may also lack your usual ardor for reading news or gossip, including the usual mayhem in the morning papers. You may be too tender to read about any type of violence, harshness, or peril, and will shy away from it for a while. The same with crass gossip. Celebrity shenanigans or a politician caught with a pole-dancing mistress can seem trivial compared to what you've been going through. But in the weeks, months, and even years after a grief, you may have a compulsive desire to read about grief.

This uptick in reading and study may have to do with the nature of books themselves and how comforting they can be. A book is, literally, something to hold on to. It makes no demands, doesn't judge, and goes at your pace. It's there waiting on the bedside table as you sleep in case you need to flick on the light and let it help you get through those awful 4:30 A.M.s. But it isn't just comfort that people seem to be after. If that were the case, they would be drawn to escapist fluff, something to take their mind off their pain. The reverse is frequently true. Grieving people tend to read to put their minds squarely *on* their pain. They "read themselves" right smack into the center of it. They start *ingesting* books, articles, stuff from the internet, spiritual matter—anything to feed the empty space in their understanding. Anything with the word "grief" grabs their attention. It's as though grieving persons are trying to make up for lost time, like cramming for a test they haven't studied for.

But, as you undertake this course of study there are certain things you may want to bear in mind.

As with many subjects, people may know certain buzzwords related to grief, and may even be familiar with ideas that have found their way into the pool of general knowledge. But often these bits of information are misguided and sometimes steer a person in the wrong direction. As Steve Martin said of philosophy, "You remember just enough to screw you up for the rest of your life." Misconceptions about grief probably won't ruin your life, but there are pitfalls to be avoided.

One of these involves the "Five Stages of Grief." You may have some awareness of them, or have at least heard of them. In looking for books on grief, you may reach for materials on the five stages because they are vaguely recognizable. As mentioned previously, the so-called five stages were developed by Elizabeth Kubler-Ross during her work with terminally ill patients.

Consequently they tend to be more useful for people dealing with that particular challenge than for people in grief.

That said, an understanding of the stages certainly can't hurt. While psychologists agree that they tend not to occur in any particular order in a dying person, it's amazing how distinct the change from one stage to another can be. What's different for those in grief is that these stages don't usually happen consecutively, they happen concurrently. If someone asks you, "Have you been through anger? Or denial? Or bargaining? Or depression? Or acceptance?" you'll probably answer, "This morning."

Grief is always messier than it's presented. Read all the psychological stuff, but understand that it's going to be put through the Cuisinart of your own grieving mind.

Avoid books that relate too specifically to your own grief. If you're a middle-aged Presbyterian male from Wisconsin who has just lost his wife, don't read a book called *Middle-Aged Presbyterian Men from Wisconsin Who've Lost Their Wives*. It may seem odd, but books that hit so close to home tend not to be helpful. You may spend the whole book thinking, "That's not how it happened," or "That's not how I felt," or "That's not how *my* wife was." The brain is on guard for faults and ignores advice that might be useful.

Finding "useful" material is the point. Most grieving people will take anything that has even a slight chance of helping them, and not only "grief books" do the trick. All sorts of reading can console, so stay open, even to the bizarre. We spoke with a man who told us that books on Twelve Step programs helped him through the loss of his mother. Joan Didion was soothed by reading Emily Post on grief. It's impossible to know what's going to strike one's subconscious fancy, so don't be too quick to dismiss anything.

One form of reading many grievers are instinctually drawn to is poetry.

Poetry seems to be able to salve something in the grieving, and there are definite reasons why. Billy Collins, an American poet laureate, has a nice theory about it. He writes:

> In times of crisis it's interesting that people don't go to the novel or say, "We should all go out to a movie," or "Ballet would help us." It's always poetry. What we want to hear is a human voice speaking in our ear.

The voice of a poet speaking into your ear can be consoling because it's usually telling you that even the most painful, gruesome moments in life can carry an air of dignity.

Appropriately, the best way to get this point across is with a poem. Galway Kinnell's "St. Francis and the Sow" describes the old saint approaching a dirty, reeking pig lying in the mud. With disregard for the animal's rancid state, Francis places his hand on the sow's head, and in doing so he tells even this foulest of creatures that it is touchable. After he lifts his hand, the poem goes on to say:

> . . . sometimes it is necessary
> to reteach a thing its loveliness,
> to put a hand on its brow
> of the flower
> and retell it in words and in touch
> it is lovely
> until it flowers again from within, of self-blessing. . .

Poets touch things that are difficult to touch, things like the indignities of grief, and in doing so, reteach them their "loveliness."

Poetry dignifies not only by acknowledging the grimiest emotions but also by ordering them. While the medium is highly expressive, it also has stringent schemes and patterns and always an extremely deliberate choice of words. Great poetry is maximum feeling combined with maximum form, and "form" is a godsend when grieving people's thoughts and emotions are so scattered. Verse organizes the clutter. These are words taken verbatim from a woman whose husband recently died:

> Peter was . . . so much . . . every single . . . my whole
> world. . . We did things . . . I was with him always. . .

Poetry takes the feelings in this raw stammering and articulates them as something more shaped. These lines by W. H. Auden were written decades before this woman lost her husband, but it's hard to imagine that they don't capture what she was trying to get across.

> He was my North, my South, my East, my West,
> My working week and my Sunday rest

Even when all the touching of dirty things and the ordering of sloppy emotions is of no relief, poetry is something powerful to hold on to when you need it. While it may not be a weapon, it can be a pretty good shield.

On the night Martin Luther King, Jr., was shot, Robert Kennedy had the unenviable task of telling an audience in Indiana, filled mostly with African Americans, the news. He walked on stage armed only with poetry and the knowledge that people were already rioting in other cities across the country. After announcing that Dr. King had been killed, Kennedy recited these lines from Aeschylus:

> In our sleep, pain which cannot forget
> falls drop by drop upon the heart
> until, in our own despair, against our will
> comes wisdom through the awful grace of God.

There were no riots in Indiana that night.

In a piercing bit of irony, Aeschylus's words would go on to mark Kennedy's own grave when he was shot and killed just two months later.

If you're not someone who normally reads poetry, try it. You don't have to be an expert; just read the words and see what sticks. Don't worry about understanding it, just feel it, as you would music. No one listens to the Beatles and says, "Wait, what's a 'hard day's night'? This stuff's over my head!" You just enjoy the sounds and rhythms and, especially, the way it makes you feel.

JUSTICE

When you hear the word "justice" connected with grief, the first image that comes to mind is a crusader, someone whose loved one has been taken from them and who seeks justice against the individual or the "system" responsible.

This sort of justice has not only consoled many grieving people, it has also been responsible for some of the most positive changes in civic society. In its strongest form, the consolation of justice has stopped criminals, created laws, changed societal protocols, educated, lobbied, heightened public awareness, launched alert systems, formed charities, and even forced municipalities to install traffic lights where there were none. In many ways, large and small, the consolation of justice has changed America. Significant changes in our history have been sparked by grief. Because of a death as the result of an injustice, people have devoted their lives to righting it—from fighting wars to struggling for civil rights to campaigning for change in our political life.

While the concept of "justice" has a moral gravity to it (none of the other eight consolations we have identified make it into the Pledge of Allegiance), it also prompts more inclusive and down-to-earth views. Smaller, everyday instances of justice can console people in grief.

Justice is a scale—it measures. It tells us when there is an imbalance. It begins with a realization that the scale is off kilter and culminates with steps to balance it. Anytime someone responds to a tragedy by changing or fixing or ad*just*ing, this is the consolation of justice.

We have famous instances of people tipping the scales as a consequence of grief. Judy and Dennis Shepard are the parents of Matthew Shepard, the openly gay young man from Laramie, Wyoming, who was killed by two homophobic local boys—one of whom was an eagle scout. The Shepards' long fight to call attention to the hate that killed their son culminated on October 28, 2009, when President Obama signed into law the Matthew Shepard Act. This act expands the 1969 federal hate-crime law to include crimes motivated by sexual orientation. It was signed eleven years after Matthew Shepard died, tied to a fence on the outskirts of his hometown.

His father had this to say a few months after the murder:

> After his death—Matt's beating, hospitalization, and funeral focused world attention on hate. Good is coming out of evil. People have said enough is enough. I miss my son, but am proud he was my son.

While the Matthew Shepard Act is a landmark in hate-crime legislation, lesser-known examples of justice happen all the time. They spring up through the small gestures of everyday people, and they right the scales nonetheless. They are exemplified by people like the Adam family, who wrote the following words to their son after he died at age twenty-three of Ewings sarcoma:

> It was astonishing how you bumbled through life somehow always getting exactly what you wanted. You faced the

hideous pain and indignity of cancer with deep grace and boundless courage. In the very face of death you made us laugh. You would be pleased to know that we have, as you wanted, established The Alex Adam Award at Princeton, for the most "talented undergrad with the lowest GPA." You would have won it in a heartbeat.

Alex and his family made sure the scales of justice will be a little less tipped against talented students with poor grade-point averages.

We heard dozens of similar tales of everyday justice, people whose grief was channeled into helping, fixing, championing. Like the forty-year-old man we got to know who lost his sister to breast cancer and signed up to run a five-kilometer race for cancer awareness. It was touching to watch this significantly out-of-shape guy lay off the cigars and forgo junk food in order to shrink his ample love handles enough to run the race in his sister's memory. It was equally hard not to hear the theme music from *Chariots of Fire* play in your head as we watched him lumber across the finish line.

People often change their own behavior because of what they have learned during grief. Very few people emerge from the ordeal of illness or grief without some soul version of a "to-do" list, peccadilloes of character they feel need tweaking, skewed priorities that need reevaluating.

Gene O'Kelly was the CEO of a major corporation who was diagnosed with a terminal illness. In his final months he made a list of some two thousand people he wanted to say good-bye to. These good-byes usually took the form of a long walk. For several people on the list, O'Kelly regretfully admitted, "it was not only the final time we would take such a leisurely walk together, but also the first."

Our scales teeter so frequently toward being too busy to notice or to share with loved ones the transcendent treats of life, things like Gene O'Kelly's walks. But no one on his death-bed looks at those closest to him and says, "I regret how often we sat by fires together" or "how many times we had cocktails under a sunset."

George Vaillant, a professor at Harvard's Medical School, has for 30 years been in charge of a psychological study of adult development. It tracks the lives of 724 subjects who, 70 years ago, agreed to be monitored for the rest of their lives. The archives of the study are a treasure trove of psychological data: thousands of interview transcripts, extensive evaluation forms, and both medical and educational records.

The focus of the study is on what Anna Freud codified as "defense mechanisms," a term for the unconscious ways that people respond to traumas and troubles. In Vaillant's words, "Life isn't easy. Terrible things happen to everyone." Vaillant, who has dedicated his life to this study, is himself the son of a father who committed suicide.

An article in the *Atlantic* explains that the central question of Vaillant's work "is not how much or how little trouble the subjects of his study met," but "precisely how—and to what effect—they responded to that trouble." Because of the wealth of data, Vaillant is able to trace the mental stratagems and per-sonal decisions that led the subjects through life and assess the outcomes.

The useful thing about Vaillant's findings for people in grief is the hierarchy of defense mechanisms he has discovered. He ranks them in order of effectiveness as proven by the lives of those in his study. As the *Atlantic* phrased it, our "defenses can spell our redemption or ruin." This is doubly so for people trying to "defend" themselves against grief.

The worst defense mechanisms, which Vaillant categorizes as "immature," include "acting out, passive aggression, hypochondria, and fantasy." Not much better than these are what he calls "neurotic" defenses. They include the "repression" of, or "disassociation" from, one's feelings.

Among the healthiest defense mechanisms, the most effective is called "sublimation," which involves finding a way to channel trauma into positive action. It's surprising how much better the lives of people who used sublimation are compared to those in the study who employed more immature or neurotic mechanisms.

George Vaillant's work is encouraging for those who are drawn to the sort of altruism that undergirds grieving people's quest for justice.

Grief can be almost diabolical in its creation of injustice. There will never be a shortage of laws to pass, races to run, behaviors to modify, or professions to be chosen in attempts to throw weight on the other side of the scale. But no one we spoke with had to heal themselves through the consolation of justice more than Suse and Peter Lowenstein.

Given what happened to them, they had a long way to go. Not only was their son taken from them (the nightmare of any parent), but it happened by violent means, and the particularly willful violence of terrorism.

Any parents would view the energy and personality of their child as the very opposite of death, but in the case of Alexander Lowenstein, age twenty-one, this could not have been more true. He had beach-bum blond hair and a skier/surfer/swimmer's body and energy. In the months before the crash he was having the time of his life studying in London.

Two weeks before the attack on his flight back to America, Suse visited him abroad, a kind of mother/son vacation. It was during this trip that Alexander told her of his decision to further his studies in psychology and "maybe someday work with kids." Suse said it was also on that trip that her son, "now quite a gentleman," had for the first time in his life "picked up the check." Pictures of their time together, taken with Alexander's camera, were recovered from the wreckage.

To lose all this in one flash of a terrorist's hate was injustice enough, but there were other instances of injustice for the Lowensteins to endure: governments ill-equipped to deal with the human factors of the crash, and an airline whose protocols and business interests trumped sensitivity to the families of Flight 103's victims.

Upon release by Scottish authorities, Alexander's body was flown back to America. When the Lowensteins went to receive their son's remains at Kennedy Airport, they were directed to a remote area adjacent to the runway, a place used to offload livestock. A grubby white truck with old graffiti on it pulled up to the loading dock where the Lowensteins stood waiting. The back door rolled open, and inside was Alexander's coffin among other crates and cargo. Baggage handlers used a forklift to take the coffin off the truck and set it down in front of the Lowensteins with a thud. The coffin had tape across it that said: *Contaminated. Do Not Open.* "That is how my son was returned to me," Suse said, "like a piece of garbage." The low-level State Department official who had accompanied them to the airport was so appalled that she burst into tears, and the Lowensteins had to help her pull herself together.

But this was 1988, and the Lowensteins were pioneers on the unforgiving terrain of losing loved ones to terrorism, terrain that has since been traveled by many others.

The man who blew up Flight 103, killing Alexander Lowenstein and 269 other people, was released from a Scottish prison on August 20, 2009. Mohmed Al Megrahi, who was terminally ill with prostate cancer, was released under a Scottish legal system that permits "compassionate release" of terminally ill prisoners. But there is much speculation that his release was part of a deal between Libya and the United Kingdom related to oil. Injustice has a way of piling on. Good people get more than they can be expected to bear without letting hatred overcome their hearts.

The families of the victims of Flight 103 had to watch as every news channel showed Migrahi's return to his native Libya, where he received a hero's welcome and an affectionate homecoming. In what might be called "perverse poetic *in*justice," the last image these families will have of the terrorist who took down PanAm Flight 103 is him coming off a plane into the arms of loved ones—something they were denied on December 21, 1988. One has to wonder how Suse is able to sublimate the hate she must feel and turn it, instead, into art and meaning and justice with her sculptor's hands.

Suse has coroner's photographs that were taken of Alexander at the morgue in Scotland. Every year or so she forces herself to take them out and look at them. When asked why she would do such a thing, she said, "My son was beautiful. When you look at the pictures of him in that morgue, he looked so ugly. Hate did that to him. Hate makes things ugly."

So each day Suse walks into her studio and gets back to work making things that are beautiful.

Just as there is heroism in the fight for justice on the battlefield, there are heroes in everyday places. Families have suffered much and fought, in their own unique ways, for justice, without succumbing to blinding hatred.

With all the subsequent folklore surrounding the Matthew Shepard case, it's easy to forget what gave the Shepards a moral high ground, what made the country, and the world, respect them. It was their decision to temper justice with mercy.

This played out on the day the two men found guilty of killing Matthew were to be sentenced. Wyoming is a state that's not afraid to employ the death penalty and, given the brutality of the crime and its national attention, a death sentence was all but assured. It was pretty much the Shepards' call to make. Here is what Dennis Shepard read to a stunned courtroom before one of his son's killers, twenty-one-year-old Aaron McKinney, was sentenced to life in prison without the possibility of parole:

> Judy has been quoted as being against the death penalty.
> It has been stated that Matt was against the death penalty.
> Both of these statements are wrong. Matt believed that
> there were crimes and incidents that justified the death
> penalty, I too believe in the death penalty. I would
> like nothing better than to see you die, Mr. McKinney.
> However, this is the time to begin the healing process. To
> show mercy to someone who refused to show any. I am
> going to grant you life, as hard as it is for me to do so,
> because of Matthew.

Many people, devastated by grief, seek justice in a less enlightened way. Justice is so powerful that it is usually the only consolation that makes even a dent in the grief of people who have had unspeakable things happen to those they love. But anything powerful can also be dangerous. This is often the case with misguided crusades for justice.

Hate must feel like justice to those in the throes of it. There are grieving people who devote themselves so ferociously to a fight that they end up hurting the people around them. So caught up are they in the all-consuming battle to avenge the death of someone they lost, they end up neglecting the people they still have. Divorces happen, families splinter.

Perhaps this is why, every year, on December 21, the anniversary of Flight 103, the Lowensteins spend the day with their younger son, their daughter-in-law, and the three grandchildren. They make it a point to do something that is fun, uplifting, consoling. This year they went to the Broadway musical *Jersey Boys*.

CHAPTER FOUR

GRIEF EXPRESSING ITSELF

SELF-NARRATIVE

Everyone has a self-narrative, a story we tell ourselves about who we are, or who we think we are. At times this narrative may be challenged, but our need to believe in it is so strong that we justify ourselves *to* ourselves, using that most impressive piece of human mental equipment: rationalization. "Cheating people? Nah, I'm just a good businessman." "Passive aggressive? Me? It's just that my family, friends, co-workers, and pets are all against me." At its best, our self-narrative mechanism is much more than a cunning inner lawyer. It also gives us faith, a sense of purpose, and a reason to get "up and at 'em" each day. In the now-famous lines of Joan Didion, "We tell ourselves stories in order to live."

We begin this chapter on "expression" with a sobering notion: grief changes our self-narrative, alters our established story of who we are, and often does so in ways that are both challenging and transformative.

Example: A spouse dies and, for the survivor, life feels sad but, strangely, *freer*. The deceased would never have done something as devil-may-care as taking a long walk after dinner for an ice cream cone, but maybe the surviving spouse does that one night and likes the way it feels. Now the person is left wondering what these new feelings say about who he or she is.

Example: Someone who cared for a dying loved one is feeling not only sad that the person is gone but also like the caregiver has been fired from his or her "job." A mother may be a kind of CEO of her only child, the executive officer of snacks, laundry, schedules, manners, dreams. A friend may have served as a full-time consultant of sorts. Where do these people "go to work" the morning after the death? They wonder what they're going to do with themselves now.

Example: A fifteen-year-old boy's best friend dies. Now the boy walks around feeling "a little bit nauseous all the time." He can't stop thinking about the way his friend looked in his coffin, and sometimes he goes online to read about the rare disease that killed him. Yesterday he broke out in a cold sweat after feeling a lump on his hipbone, until he remembered conking it on a folding chair trying to keep a basketball in bounds. He wonders if he will be, for the rest of his life, a scared person.

Example: A married couple, both academics, are together twelve years when the woman unexpectedly dies. The husband not only can't believe how diminished he feels without his partner (that's what they called each other), but finds that nothing he has ever learned (or taught) is helping now. One night he downloads Dolly Parton's recording of "I Will Always Love You" and comes to the conclusion that it's actually a greater work of art than Ovid's *Metamorphosis*. He wonders if his life of study has come to mean nothing.

Example: The daughter whose mother was so perfect she'd make Martha Stewart look like Ma Kettle, or the son whose father was so formidable he'd make John Wayne seem like a French actor. Both children love their parents very much, but after they die the two can't help but feel that something in them has shifted for the better. The psychotherapist Jeanne

Safer wrote a book about this feeling. It explores, as stated by the subtitle, "How Losing a Parent Can Change an Adult's Life—for the Better." The book is called _Death Benefits_, and on the jacket is a picture of a bird flying out of a cage. (If your folks have passed, you may want to read this book. If they are still living, you may want to leave a copy of it on your coffee table during their next visit and see how that goes.) The son and daughter wonder what this means about how they felt toward their parents all along.

All the people in these examples are struggling with the same issue. They are coming to realize that their relationship to the person who died is not just one thing. All relationships, grief or not, are a ratio of different aspects. Nine-tenths of the mother adores her youngest child, but one-tenth knows that if she'd stopped having kids after the first two, she and her husband could have retired to the lake house by now. Four-fifths of the brother is thrilled that his sister got an impressive job, but one-fifth knows it will put more family pressure on him to pull himself together. Two-thirds of a friend is happy about another friend's hot new love, but one-third is tired of spending hours on Match.com and wishes the love gods had smiled on him instead. Three-quarters of a person volunteers in the soup kitchen because she knows there are unfortunate people who need help, but one-quarter likes to be able to tell people that she volunteers in a soup kitchen.

Most people prefer a self-narrative that tells them they are 100 percent one thing or another. Strong truths that shave a point or two seem unattractive. But the unattractive truths that come to light during grief are not only strong, they are new. Strong truths are hard enough to keep down; strong _new_ truths are bound to slip the leash and begin expressing themselves, like it or not.

One of the psychological perks of grief is that it brings you back to an understanding of ambiguity, reminds you that the truth of life is never just one thing but at least two, usually more. Grief not only changes your self-narrative, it changes your narrative about life itself.

After experiencing a major death, life will never again be unambiguous. It can never be "just *one* thing" again, not after you know that "it" can happen to you. Not after you learn that life as you knew it can stop on a dime. "Funeral Blues" echoes again: *I thought our love would last forever: I was wrong.*

Once you have experienced the crisis that causes a major grief, there is a point of demarcation in your life's calendar, a "before and after" notch. BC: before the crisis; AD: after the death of someone you love. That date divides your life. Each year you'll know when you reach that day. Every time you look at a photograph you'll find yourself thinking things like, "That was me before I knew," "This is at the ball game a few months before his last time in the hospital," "That's Thanksgiving after the summer of the accident." Even if the picture doesn't concern you, your friend will show you him and his girlfriend at a New Year's Eve party, both wearing huge "2006!" glasses, and you'll say "Great picture"—but you'll think, "Worst year of my life."

Ambiguity is a new normal of grieving, and if you cannot teach yourself to accept it you will have a much harder time dealing with grief. Those who seem to do best at this use grief as a chance to integrate ambiguity into their self-narrative.

This is the point of many self-help (*"You Can Be Great!"*) seminars, where the (highly paid) motivational speaker says, "Every crisis is an opportunity in disguise!" To which a grieving person might say, "Good disguise." A "crisis" might be an opportunity if you are being paid ten thousand dollars a day to lead seminars about it, but to those down in the muck of grief, coming up with a new self-narrative is such grunt work that only someone like Yeats can describe the scene:

> Now that my ladder's gone,
> I must lie down where all the ladders start
> In the foul rag-and-bone shop of the heart.

Grief is that foul rag-and-bone shop of the heart. And the two foulest items you must integrate into the postgrief "you" are (1) guilt and (2) self-pity—two forces that are fraught with ambiguity and that can both affect your self-narrative.

David Rieff, who was responsible for the care of his mother, Susan Sontag, at the end of her life, calls guilt "the default position of the survivor." This happens because of so many "unanswerable questions," like, "Did I do the right thing? Could I have done more?" And this self-doubt and self-scrunity stretch well beyond those directly responsible for someone's care. They extend, at least in an unconscious way, to anyone who loved the deceased. As absurd as it may sound, when someone you love dies, it's a huge blow to your self-esteem because it means that *you* were not enough to keep them alive.

Rieff says about his mother, "In the end all we had was love, and that was not enough." He acknowledges that Sontag appreciated that love.

> Nonetheless, the stark truth is that love was no consolation to her as she fought so desperately for her life. And in the end, those who loved her failed her as the living always fail the dying, for we could not actually do the thing she really wanted, which was to stave off extinction for just some time longer.

Dying people appreciate the love of those who are "there for them," but they too know it won't be enough. You can see that they know it. If someone dies suddenly, you feel that somehow, somewhere retroactively, they knew you weren't up to saving them. No matter how much you loved them, it wasn't enough to keep them from turning down the street on which they were killed, or enough to have taken them to the doctor earlier, even though nothing was wrong at the time. This guilt can be a blow to one's sense of self, even if the feelings occur on an unconscious level.

Of course, not everyone goes through this guilt-induced self-doubt. Plenty of people do the opposite: they turn the page, no problem. We met one woman, quite a character, whose grown children were upset when, only a few months after her husband of twenty-five years died, she put on a mini-skirt and headed for a bar. She told her kids, "Hey, I swore to love him 'till death do us part.' And death did us part. So now I'm goin' out!" Her children, like so many grieving people, had trouble thinking ambiguously. To them, their mother's role was *only* as "dad's wife." They could not compute that her life might have a second act.

Guilt can be paradoxical in this way—which is just a high-brow way of saying that guilt knows how to torture a grieving person from just about every possible angle. Grieving people, on the one hand, feel guilty about *not* getting on with their lives; but when they finally do get on with them, they feel guilty about being "okay" without the person they lost. And when you are struggling with guilt, loved ones are often at the ready to help you feel worse about yourself.

The second big-ticket item in a grieving person's self-narrative is *self-pity.* Joan Didion already had this issue in her crosshairs just days after her husband died. She turned on her computer and wrote these four stark lines:

Life changes fast.
Life changes in the instant.
You sit down to dinner and life as you know it changes.
The question of self-pity.

This is how her book begins: a cluster of four blunt lines, set off from the rest of the text. What's fascinating about these lines is not that they were quoted in most of the reviews and articles about the book, but that those who quoted them frequently left off the last line. Self-pity is a topic so distasteful that people accidentally-on-purpose forget to mention it. But in her book Didion doesn't.

In the oft-neglected last line, notice that she says, "the question." As if it were a choice. People in grief actually do make a choice about how much self-pity they will allow themselves. It's easy to permit a loss to take your self-narrative in a self-pitying direction, to think of yourself as the lead in a tragic drama or epic novel, to view the bad things that have happened to you as messages sent by life itself. Grief can permeate the story of a whole life, can become an uber-allegory for the "crappiness" of it, one big metaphor for every disappointment from kindergarten to the present.

A *New Yorker* cartoon shows a man in the hospital. He's propped up uncomfortably in a bed with tubes and wires connecting him to all sorts of medical machinery, and he's wincing in considerable pain. His wife is standing at the foot of his bed wearing her coat and carrying her purse. Beholding the awful scene, she says, "I can't believe this is happening to me."

Some people are grief hogs, grief narcissists—grief, they think, is all about them, and, worse than that, *they* are all about grief. A character in *Anna Karenina* introduces himself by saying, "You are acquainted with my grief?" Some allow grief to change their first name from "Ann" or "Joe" to "Poor," so that friends will say, "Let's invite poor Ann to the party," or "What does poor Joe do on Valentine's Day? Wishes he was dead, I guess."

You might be edging toward this situation if you catch yourself "tallying." This is when you take every bad thing that happens throughout the day and apply it to your already impressively high stack of woe. It's an easy thing for grieving people to fall into. You crack your shin on the coffee table and exclaim, "Great! I'm a widow *and* I hurt my shin!" Your car stalls and you say, "More death!" Your computer crashes and you think, "Cancer of the hard drive!" You accidentally ruin a sweater in the wash, and you sit on the floor of the laundry room holding it like *The Pietà*.

When something bad happens, people are prone to asking, "Why me?" When something good happens, the question rarely arises. We assume the good things are deserved. After forty years as one of America's best character actors, Charles Durning at long last won a Tony Award for his performance in a revival of *Cat on a Hot Tin Roof.* In his acceptance speech he said, "I don't deserve this." Then he paused and added, "But last year I had cancer and I didn't deserve that either." That's a man at peace with ambiguity, and a fine old thespian like him probably knows it makes for a richer and more nuanced tale.

Each griever must ask the question, "Who am I, now that you're gone?" And the answer to that question often revises one's self-narrative. Grief is a story you tell yourself. It's a story of the *death* of someone you loved. It's a story of the *life* of someone you loved. It's a story of your life *with* them, and it's a story of your life *without* them. Grief is a story you tell yourself—but you have a collaborator. The feelings unleashed by the death of someone you loved will keep putting in their two cents. Get used to it.

MEN

A twenty-one-year-old man's sister died in a car accident. At the time the young man lived in the same city as his uncle. The city was a three-hour drive from where his parents lived, so when the tragic news hit, it was decided that the uncle would drive the brother home. For the entirety of the three-hour trip, the uncle hardly said a word. No tears, no emotion, no discussion. Just tense silence. The young man told us that ride was probably the most uncomfortable few hours of his life.

This story makes you wonder how an older man, placed in a situation where a young person could use a little warmth, could fail so clearly to step up to the plate. The uncle wasn't able to give any counsel, show any affection, or even talk to a young man whose sister had just died.

But there's more to the story. This uncle, it turns out, did more for the family than most people would ever have been able to. For one thing, he identified the girl's body. He did not want her parents to have to do that. Seeing what he saw, he made the decision that the parents should not see the girl at all. He made further arrangements with the funeral parlor for the family to have some time with her, alone, in a private room with a closed casket. He made every phone call and assumed all the administrative responsibilities that would normally have been handled by the girl's father, his brother-in-law, who was too shattered to do much of anything.

Amazingly, the uncle had done much of this work before he even picked up his nephew. At the awful onset of the accident, the uncle had driven the three hours to the family's home to be with his sister and brother-in-law. This was when he identified the body and began dealing with some of the clerical issues that needed attention. He then drove three hours back to the city to pick up his nephew.

This story illustrates two facets of men's behavior. First, men often put their feelings into actions rather than words. And, second, they often get a bum rap for doing so.

Men are not always able, or willing, to engage in kitchen table psychotherapy. They just aren't. Men often express themselves as much in their silence as they do in their words. Robert Bly wrote a poem called "Some Men Find it Hard to Finish Sentences" about how men keep everything inside, which he illustrates by having the entire poem consist of unfinished sentences, the last one being: "There's a lot to . . ."

"A lot to" *what*? What is it the man needs to do in his silence—a silence that can frustrate loved ones who might view his unfinished sentences as a lack of feeling?

What a man does—in what looks like heartless silence and reserved resolve—is try to keep himself ready in case something needs to be done, fixed, helped, protected, saved. There are plenty of times in life when there's a tough job to be done, and it helps to have a tough guy on hand to do it. When your tire needs changing, you don't think to yourself, "Gee, I wish there were a grief counselor around to help me!"

These days men get a lot of cultural pressure to be less forceful and more sensitive. We live in a time where men are often shamed for expressing masculine instincts. A kindergarten boy who gets in a tussle at recess may be hauled before a kangaroo court of teachers, counselors, parents, and probably pharmacists, only to emerge with the belief that aggression in any form is aberrant. Twelve years later when his parents are trying to get him into Yale, they'll wonder why he's not assertive and refuses to approach his SATs as a chance to smash his competition, the way mom and dad would like him to.

We live in a time when, for men, telling a dirty joke is thought of as a sex crime, raising his voice as an assault, and zoning out during one of his girlfriend's harangues as evidence that he's Satan. In turn, men get their revenge by making sure all advertisers and media makers know that men have now been rendered so insecure that the only type of woman they will find attractive is one who is under a hundred pounds, has the vocal timbre of Marilyn Monroe, the IQ of a mannequin, and lips cosmetically engineered into a permanent pucker.

While sex roles may be in a state of cultural flux, at a time of grief men default to something more innate—and far less politically correct! Recent societal and academic pressures have made it taboo to claim inherent gender differences. A statement like "Men are good at protecting and women good at caring for" would be dismissed by most sociology professors as reductive and behind the times.

But grief *is* reductive and behind the times.

Grief pulls people back into a deeper, more intuitive, caveman/cavewoman way of responding. When tragedy hits, these primal instincts begin to surface. Men start protecting, and woman start caring.

This is not to say that men are unfeeling. Just because they don't talk about some things doesn't mean they don't feel them. The movie *In the Bedroom* takes place in a Northeast fishing town where the men are pretty sturdy, with weathered faces and homespun accents. In one scene the father whose son has died is back at his regular poker game, playing for the first time since the boy was murdered. Everyone is uncomfortable and all but silent. His poker buddies don't know what to say, or if they should say something about not having anything to say. The father finally can't take it anymore. He blurts out: "Say something, for Christ sake! Quit pussyfooting around me!" After a pause, the men look to an older man who is something of the town poet. The old codger, still holding his poker hand, recites from Longfellow's "My Lost Youth":

> There are things of which I may not speak;
> There are dreams that cannot die;

There are thoughts that make the strong heart weak,
And bring a pallor to the cheek,
And a mist before the eye.
And the words of that fatal song
Come over me like a chill:
"A boy's will is the wind's will,
And the thoughts of youth are long, long thoughts."

When he's done reciting, the father says calmly, "Now let's play." And they do.

That's how a lot of men do it. They try to get "the moment" out of the way as soon as possible in order to get on with things. And it's not just older men in fishing towns who do that. A college boy who had lost his brother decided to get a tattoo of his deceased brother's initials on his arm. Because he was a private person, the tattoo was small and placed on his inner wrist so his watch could conceal it most of the time. One night he was at a bar with a bunch of his male friends. When he lifted a beer, a friend noticed the tattoo and asked about it. The boy told us what happened next:

> I told the guys what the tattoo was, and everyone got kinda quiet and weird for a second. But then someone said we should do a toast to my brother. And people said a few nice things about him and about me being his brother and then we toasted. That was it. We just went back to drinking and watching the game and no one talked about it again.

Guys are guys when it comes to grief, a fact that is not subject to the cultural pressures of the time. Death walks through the door, and something old expresses itself inside people. There's a word for it: atavistic, meaning a feeling that seems to come from your ancestors. Because grief comes strong and without warning, it's more of an atavism than we realize. Still, people read male reticence as a lack of feeling.

It might help if we thought of expressions of feeling and affection, whether in word, gesture, or emotional openness, as *currency*. Different people's expressions have different values. If Richard Simmons says you played "a terrific game," it's not the same as if Vince Lombardi says it. We all know people whose expressive "currency" suffers from inflation, people who sign off every phone call, letter, and e-mail with "I luv ya." There's nothing wrong with this, but just convert the "exchange rate" in your head when dealing with such people, allowing for inflation.

For many men emotional expression is more "costly" and should, thus, be considered more valuable. In a picture of a cemetery in Normandy, where many American soldiers who died in the D-day invasion are buried, you can see a card on one of the headstones that reads: *From your brother, Pete. I remember you.* No flowers, balloons, pictures, or purple language. Just, "I remember you." But in the emotional exchange rate, that's worth a lot coming from an eighty-two-year-old man from the Plains states.

Some people never hear their father say, "I love you," so when one of these dads can muster it up in a time of grief, it should mean a lot. The father of a thirty-seven-year-old man died after a long illness. A day before he died, the father said, "I have one big regret in life." When the son asked what it was, the father said, "After you lost that playoff game your senior year in high school I should have gone up and given you a hug." To an outsider that may not seem like much, but to the son it was worth a million bucks.

Aside from gestures and words of affection, another big issue for men is crying. Many men perceive crying as a weakness. This is understandable when you consider how people describe crying—we say "I fell apart," "I broke down," "I lost it," "I burst into tears." Falling, breaking, losing, and bursting are not qualities that most men are comfortable having. They consider crying in front of others as embarrassing. Doing it in public feels inappropriate.

While no man should force emotion, he shouldn't feel the need to suppress it either. Even tears. Norman Schwarzkopf, commander of coalition forces in the 1991 Gulf War, once said, "I would never trust any man who cannot cry." If feeling is currency, there's no need to be miserly. If you don't feel like crying, don't. But if you do feel like crying, don't force yourself not to. Sometimes it's good for your loved ones, even helpful, to see a man cry. In the loosely autobiographical novel *A Happy Marriage*, Rafael Yglesias writes as a husband whose wife has a terminal disease. In one scene the woman's family gathers to be with her, and everyone makes an effort not to cry:

> They were trying very hard not to weep, presumably in the belief their tears would make Margaret feel worse, although they would, in fact, have made her feel loved.

Intentionally holding back tears doesn't always make the people around you think you are strong. Sometimes it makes them feel unloved.

One final story:

In 1966 in suburban New Jersey, two men from adjacent towns both worked in New York City and carpooled each morning to the bus station. They were blue-collar guys who had worked their way up to white-collar jobs.

One day, coming home from work, they got off the bus to find one man's sister waiting in the station parking lot. Tragic news: his five-year-old son had drowned in the family's above-ground pool.

That night his car-pool buddy couldn't get the scene out of his head. Imagining his friend at home with his wife, staring at that pool in the backyard, was a haunting thought. When he called the friend's house, he found that the sight of the pool *was* too much for the man and his wife to take, so they were staying with relatives.

The next morning, at the crack of dawn, the buddy began making phone calls. By 8 A.M. all the men in the neighborhood had been gathered, a group consisting of a carpenter, an electrician, an elevator repairman, and a machinist. These were typical 1966 New Jersey guys—good with their hands, decent, probably drank too much on weekends. Lugging their toolboxes, they stopped at a hardware store and a landscaping nursery, then drove to the home of the man whose child had drowned.

They spent the early hours of the day dismantling the pool, draining it, and hauling it away to a junkyard. They spent the rest of the afternoon laying sod, putting down crushed stone, planting the flowers they bought at the nursery, and setting a flagstone path. No one talked about the drowning, only about which tools were best to use and how to spread the sod evenly. When the husband and wife came home the next day, the pool was gone, and in its place was a garden.

Now fade out, and fade in forty years later. By this time, with job changes and family relocations, the two men no longer car-pooled and saw each other only rarely. One work reunion and an occasional Christmas card, but not much contact.

In the intervening years the couple who had lost their son had another child, also a boy. He grew up to be an outstanding young man, married, with one child and another on the way. He was a fireman in New Jersey, and though he was not injured on 9/11, he saw horrible things at Ground Zero that he couldn't shake. He sunk into a depression and, tragically, committed suicide.

When his parents heard the tragic news, one of the first calls they made, completely out of the blue, was to the old carpool buddy. Something in the couple pulled them back to that first tragedy with the pool, and they reached out for the man who had been there for them on the earlier occasion. Most of the men who helped with the pool had since died, but the carpool buddy seemed like the right person to call.

Sometimes it's good to have a man around.

WOMEN

It's Mother's Day. A husband and two young children are downstairs in the kitchen preparing breakfast while mom is upstairs sleeping (not that she can sleep with the racket that's going on down there). When the big moment comes, her bedroom door swings open and, after much fanfare on dad and the kids' part, and lots of "ooohs" and "aahhs" on her part, a tray is set before her. On it is a huge discus of partially cooked waffle batter, two pieces of incinerated bacon, a cup of coffee strong enough for a Bedouin, and a vase holding a flower that looks suspiciously like it might belong to the (very expensive) silk flower arrangement on the dining room table. After thanking her husband and kids for spoiling her so, trouper that she is, mom makes a show of sampling the breakfast riches before her. Dad and the kids high-five over their triumph and then leave for a day of go-cart racing. Ten minutes later mom is downstairs cleaning the ransacked kitchen.

What a lucky gal!

We begin with this scene because it is a nice allegory for what happens to women in a time of grief. People mean well, care a lot, but when it comes down to it, she's the only one who can clean up the mess.

Women, from grandmothers to mothers with children to high school girls, are the linchpins that hold a family together. Whether it's a nuclear family or just a circle of friends, it's rare for "the string around the bundle" not to be a woman. Everyone in the group knows that as long as *she* keeps things together they will stay that way.

And the idea that she won't is unthinkable.

Almost every great American playwright, from Arthur Miller to Tennessee Williams to Sam Shepard, has written a family drama centered on a faltering father. Only Eugene O'Neill writes about a mother who is completely unable to function. His play, *Long Day's Journey into Night*, is considered one of the greatest and certainly the most wrenching American drama. The fact that the play is almost wholly autobiographical (just compare O'Neill's detailed set descriptions to the actual O'Neill home still standing in New London, Connecticut) also gives it an eerie emotional legitimacy.

Long Day's Journey occupies its own echelon of grief in American drama. None of the other great American plays can touch it when it comes to despair. At the end of *Death of a Salesman*, Linda, the matriarch, is still standing at the grave of her dead husband, attempting to hold herself and everything else together. At the end of *Cat on a Hot Tin Roof* we know that Big Mama will be left calling the shots on the plantation long after Big Daddy is dead and gone. But at the end of *Long Day's Journey into Night*, Mary, the mother, obliterated by morphine, stands holding her wedding dress (a harrowing and grotesquely sad image) while her husband and two sons wait in neutral corners of hopelessness as the curtain falls.

American culture honors and mourns its lost fathers, but a lost mother finishes us.

American women seem to have an intuitive sense of this, so when tragedy strikes and grief abounds, they get to work saving the day, regardless of the cost to themselves.

Like the mother chipping waffle batter off the stove knobs, women throughout history have been cleaning up after men—which is to say, burying our dead. The American holiday Mother's Day was originally called Mothers' Day for Peace, and was largely the idea of the abolitionist, suffragette, and poet Julia Ward Howe. (She also wrote the lyrics for the "Battle Hymn of the Republic.") Her 1870 poem "Mothers' Day Proclamation" is considered the unofficial founding document of the holiday. She wrote it in the wake of the Civil War as a call for all women to come together as a force for peace.

While Mother's Day, as we call it, has evolved and is now commercialized into the day when it's hardest to get a reservation at a good restaurant, its roots are a grieving outcry against the loss of children in war. As Howe's "Proclamation" so poignantly states:

Our sons shall not be taken from us to unlearn
All that we have been able to teach them
Of charity, mercy, patience.

And just to show, on a smaller scale, what kind of mother Howe was, her "Proclamation," along with many of her poems, was written in complete darkness, a skill she taught herself to keep from waking her infant children.

This is what women do that men often can't. Women can make it work. If it means something as seemingly impossible as writing poetry in the dark for the sake of their children's sleep, women make it work. They become such naturals at doing so, that when a death happens, everyone else *assumes* that the women will "make it work." It's *expected* that they'll be good at feeling, caring, checking up on, picking up the slack, and attending to any wobbles in the family equipoise.

If a woman lives up to all these expectations, even at great personal sacrifice, she will not be extolled or sainted for it. People will merely think, "She's good at that kind of stuff." If, however, she comes up short, not only will she feel responsible for the undoing of people she loves, but they will most certainly blame her as they scatter to the four winds. Default blame often goes her way. There's a nasty old British expression, "A woman's place is in the wrong."

Whether or not women live up to the expectations placed on them in times of grief, they tend not to be treated equally to men. Grief too has a "glass ceiling." When a woman is suffering from grief she is met with an initial outpouring of love, support, and camaraderie. But what happens next is another version of the Mother's Day breakfast. Life returns to normal pretty quickly for everyone else, and it's assumed the woman will keep together what she's always kept together: her family, her parents' family, her siblings, her circle of friends, and a clique of colleagues.

If a grieving man goes beyond his normal sex role, he is idolized in a way that is rarely true for women. A recently widowed mother shows up to every one of her twelve-year-old son's basketball games, and no one bats an eye. But let a new widower make his kids sandwiches for school, and producers from the Lifetime Network will swoop in to buy the rights for a TV movie called *Love Is a Lunchbox*.

As men await their accolades for even the slightest gesture, women are left on the sidelines to deal with the truly down-and-dirty aspects of grief. This can mean confronting some pretty gruesome situations.

But women can take even "gruesome" and make it work. Women have an amazing capacity for facing the physical horrors of illness, tragedy, and death. They don't shy away from bodies the way men do. Women let the emotional needs of the situation override whatever grotesquery there might be; they remain physically and emotionally *present* for those who need their care, regardless of the mess.

Some of this has to do with basic physicality. Men are generally squeamish about bodies; they can go years without setting foot in a doctor's office. To a man, his body is something he uses to play sports and fill out a dress shirt, and as for the bodies of his kids, well, they're just those things that fill up diapers for a few years and then, magically, stop. Women, on the other hand, tend to have a much more mature understanding of their bodies and the bodies of their children.

Women's instinct to remain present in the direst situations is something they possess, albeit in less developed forms, from early on. We saw this impulse play itself out in the way high-school-aged women react to tragedy. Girls of that age can be self-effacing, inward, and hesitant about grabbing at the world, but they become quite different in a time of grief. Something in them rises to the occasion. Their arms seem to grow twice as long, allowing them to reach out and pull entire groups of people into an embrace. And they don't hug head to head. A girl will let the head of the person she's hugging rest lower than hers, enveloping the person with presence and protection.

Oddly, we noticed that the exact opposite tends to happen with young men. The physical carriage of boys that age is normally very confident, the world is their oyster. But when grief strikes their swagger implodes. They go inward, the eyes look down, their arms fold.

As women grow older, this "instinct of presence" pairs with an extraordinary courage, allowing them to stay in the most horrific situations as long as there is someone they must care for. It's unbelievable how far this can go.

In *How We Die*, Sherwin Nuland describes the death of Katie, a nine-year-old girl. She was stabbed to death by a complete stranger, a middle-aged paranoid schizophrenic who happened to grab her at a street fair in the middle of the day. Katie's mother witnessed the entire scene, and describes holding her daughter's lifeless body after the murderer had been restrained.

> She was gazing at me and beyond me. . . There was no look of pain in her eyes, but instead it was a look of surprise. . . We once had a portrait of her made, and it's the same look in her eyes. They were wide but not in a state of terror—it almost looked like innocence—an innocent release. As her mother, amidst all of that blood and everything else, it was actually soothing to look into her eyes. Even though she was unconscious, I felt that somehow she knew I was there, that her mother was there when she was dying. I brought her into the world and I was there when she was leaving it—in spite of the terror and horror of it, I was there.

Not only are women able to be in a situation like this, an atavistic urge in them cries out: if something terrible must happen to someone I love, I will be there. I will *choose* to be there.

Women who are not present for the death of a loved one seem to have a much harder time with grief than women who are. Those who were not "there" feel guilty for their absence, and, as a method of working through their grief, they often seek ways of returning to the death, if only in an imaginative form. This is something few men would ever dare do.

No men did so in the case of *Dark Elegy*, Suse Lowenstein's series of statues of those who lost loved ones on PanAm Flight 103. But for seventy-six women, the "instinct of presence" was so strong that they painfully relived the events and emotions of December 21, 1988, to see them memorialized in a work of art.

In 2007 a request was made to the Department of the Interior to have *Dark Elegy* bronzed and moved to Washington, D.C., as a "Memorial to All Victims of Terrorism." The deciding panel was composed entirely of men—wonkish government bureaucrats. The proposal was voted down because, according to the committee, "though a monument to victims of terrorism is a fine idea," they were looking for something "more benign."

It's not surprising that these men would not understand the instinct, the urge, and the eventual comfort of being able to say, *"I felt that somehow she knew I was there, that her mother was there when she was dying."* Nor could they understand the inner call to return to such events. Men usually do not wish to go back.

Going back, however, may be the only way some people find their way out of grief. In a *New York Times* article by Fran Schumer, Dr. Katherine Shear of Columbia University explains that grieving people may fall into a "loop of suffering." Dr. Shear refers to this loop as "complicated grief," the symptoms of which, though informally defined, include, "yearning for the loved one so intense that it strips a person of other desires. Life has no meaning; joy is out of bounds."

To combat "complicated grief," Dr. Shear developed a sixteen-week course of treatment. A crucial phase of the treatment, borrowed from the cognitive behavioral therapy used to treat victims of post-traumatic stress disorder, requires the patient to recall the death in detail while the therapist records the session. The patient must replay the tape at home, daily. The goal is to show that grief, like the tape, can be picked up or put away.

In 2005 Dr. Shear presented evidence to the *Journal of the American Medical Association* that "the treatment was twice as effective as the traditional interpersonal therapy used to treat depression or bereavement." Dr. Shear's treatment confirms what grieving women have understood all along, that going back helps.

Joan Didion went back to the death of her thirty-nine-year-old daughter, Quintana, in her stage adaptation of *The Year of Magical Thinking*. Didion's memoir of the same title was completed a year before Quintana died, so there is no mention of her death in the book. When asked by the publisher if she would like to revise the manuscript to include Quintana's death, Didion declined.

When producer Scott Rudin then approached Didion with the idea of doing *The Year of Magical Thinking* as a one-woman show, with Vanessa Redgrave playing the role, Didion could have easily just tinkered with the book enough to put it in play form. But she chose to go back to Quintana's death in a way she was not yet ready to do in her book. While about half the play is straight from the book, the other half is a painful revisiting of her daughter's death. Director David Hare said that when Redgrave read the script aloud for the first time, Didion was "absolutely shattered."

But the play and the performance were breathtaking. The whole evening was Redgrave, alone onstage, speaking directly to the audience. She is one of those actresses who seems to make eye contact with an entire room, and she gave the piece a feeling of immediacy and intimacy.

The Year of Magical Thinking closed on August 25, 2007, but on April 27, 2009, Redgrave agreed to give a one-night-only benefit performance of the play, the proceeds of which would go to UNICEF—a charity for which Julia Ward Howe, if she were alive today, might be composing proclamations.

The benefit performance, however, was canceled. Just weeks before the show, Redgrave's daughter, the actress Natasha Richardson, suffered a severe head injury while skiing in Canada. Three days later, after being flown to New York's Lenox Hill

Hospital, Richardson was removed from life support. She left behind her husband of fifteen years (actor Liam Neeson) and their two young boys. Redgrave sang her daughter a lullaby as she died.

In the months after Richardson's death, Redgrave made it clear that she wanted no special treatment or distinction for her grief as a mother. "All this talk that I am the matriarch of our family is utter rubbish," she said, "because my heart is just as damaged as those of younger members." This shifting of focus away from themselves and onto the care of others is typical in women, particularly mothers.

The benefit performance that was to happen in April was rescheduled for eight months later. On October 26, 2009, Vanessa Redgrave got back up on stage and said the words Joan Didion wrote about the death of a daughter.

> I have a few more questions I need to ask her.
> Did I lie to you?
> Did I lie to you all your life?
> When I said you're safe, I am here, was that a lie or did you believe it?

RELIGION

Grief makes many people transform their feelings about religion. It causes some people to lose it, others to get it, and still others to adjust their degree of commitment.

We are a culture in which people's religious beliefs run a large gamut, even within a single family. (The Catholic grandfather to his grandson who's in the nondenominational church: "You still going to that fake church?") The gamut runs from those who are members of a specific religion to those with a personal spirituality outside of any established religion, to those who have always been religious non-starters.

Among those who are religious, there are different degrees of commitment and intensity. On the one hand are the stalwarts—die-hard members of a religion who follow it to the letter, the sort of people who believe that "The Pearly Gates are actual gates. And they have real pearls on them. End of discussion!" On the other hand are those for whom religion is an important part of life, culture, and family, even though they are not always observant. These are the people who attend the shortest Sunday service during football season, or who go to church only for a baptism, a wedding, or a funeral—the kind of people that one priest referred to as "hatch, match, and dispatch Catholics."

Even among those who are not "traditionally" religious, one finds wide variation. Some refer to themselves as "spiritual" and are nourished by a variety of rituals and writings and an amalgam of religious ideas. (The sort of people who get married at waterfalls.) At the other end are those who vociferously oppose all religion. (The sort of people who might protest having a manger scene on the town's post office lawn.)

Often people who once thought they were unflappable on the subject begin wavering as new feelings rise up in them, feelings they cannot deny. The most intense version of this experience occurs when a person of strong religious belief is struck by grief and loses faith. Soon after the death of his wife, C. S. Lewis's writings turned to the question of faith.

> Meanwhile, where is God? This is one of the most
> disquieting symptoms . . . go to him when your need is
> desperate, when all other help is vain, and what do you
> find? A door slammed in our face, and a sound of bolting
> and double bolting on the inside. After that, silence. You
> may as well turn away. The longer you wait, the more
> emphatic the silence will become. There are no lights in

the windows. It might be an empty house. Was it ever inhabited?

Loss of faith feels this way, as deeply wounding as being betrayed by a parent, being sent away to wander on one's own. For the most devout, losing faith can feel like losing everything.

In Elie Wiesel's book *Night* he discusses how tiny scraps of faith kept the prisoners of concentration camps from succumbing to the utter horror of their lives. But even those scraps were difficult to hang on to. Wiesel describes a rabbi, "a bent old man, whose lips were always trembling," who, try as he might, could not cling to his faith.

> He used to pray all the time, in the block, in the yard, in the ranks. He would recite whole pages of the Talmud from memory, argue with himself, ask himself questions and answer himself. And one day he said to me: "It's the end. God is no longer with us. . . . I know. One has no right to say things like that. I know. . . . But what can I do? I'm not a sage, one of the elect, nor a saint. I'm just an ordinary creature of flesh and blood. I've got eyes, too, and I can see what they're doing here. Where is the Mercy? Where is God? How can I believe, how could anyone believe, in this merciful God?"

Wiesel writes of another man, Akiba Drumer, whose loss of faith left him with little reason to go on.

> . . . as soon as he felt the first cracks forming in his faith, he had lost his reason for struggling and had begun to die. . . . All he asked of us was: "In three days I shall no longer be here . . . say the Kaddish for me." We promised him.

While there is no question that some people lose their faith completely, it's much more common that people grapple with it, sometimes emerging with a faith that's deeper, more real. People for whom religion once meant Sunday suits, charity bazaars, and catching up with friends in the parking lot find that their faith stays with them as they descend into some of the darker places grief can take a person. This experience was captured by the poet Jane Kenyon in this striking little verse she wrote as she underwent treatment for a terminal cancer:

> The God of curved space, the dry
> God, is not going to help us, but the son
> Whose blood spattered
> The hem of his mother's robe.

Many people talked about a similar experience. Where religion had been an abstraction—"a God of curved space," as Kenyon says—in the face of suffering their faith became more real, more tactile, less aloof from the messy reality of true suffering. One person told us that she took great comfort from the words said by Jesus in the gospel story of the Crucifixion. The second-to-last thing he says before dying is: "My God, My God, why have you forsaken me?" Her point was that, if Jesus could feel abandoned by God in His suffering, she could forgive herself for feeling that way in a time of painful grief. A tragedy had brought her to the lowest point in her life, but once there she found that the sacred writings of her faith had descended to the dark place with her, and she emerged with her faith strengthened.

The classic texts of religions are able to put universal human feelings into beautiful words that span centuries. The words that woman quoted, for example, "Why have you forsaken me?" appear in the Old Testament, in Psalm 22, written centuries before Christ. And these words have no doubt been uttered for centuries after Christ by people all over the world, even if only paraphrased by countless common souls in the crucible of suffering. "Why have you forsaken me?"

The most enduring words of many people's religions are the prayers they have been taught. Prayers are of particular value to people in a time of crisis. In the mind-scrambling time of grief, or any crisis, you have a familiar arrangement of words at the ready. The accepted prayers of the major religions tend to be eloquent and articulate, which is why it sounds so silly when the town little league team is at a restaurant with their heads bowed and the coach ad-libs, "Lord we thank you for this fellowship today, and the blessing of this pizza with the pepperoni."

When the going gets rough, people are comforted by having an established, usually memorized prayer to reach for. It's often the last thing one can reach for in a dire time. When Akiba Drumer finally lost his faith to the relentless torment of life in a concentration camp, he still asked that a prayer be said for him. He made his friends promise to say the Kaddish. And even though the friends were in no condition to say it, and would, as Wiesel admits, eventually forget to do so, they nonetheless promised Akiba a prayer. For religious people, prayer is the last thing standing, the last thing they have. Thus the expression, "Hasn't got a prayer."

If you are grieving, those around you are drawn to express their sympathy in some way that is sacred. This is where, if you are religious, prayer can be so helpful. They can always say, "I'll pray for you." One woman, a grandmother, kept a "to pray for" list on her refrigerator. When her grandson asked, "Why are some of the names crossed off? Did they get better?" she answered, "No, they died."

Nonreligious people have the same urge toward sacred expressions of compassion, but they don't have the convenience of memorized prayers. They must come up with other versions of "praying for people." Simone Weil thought that "absolutely unmixed attention is prayer." This can mean something as simple as lighting a candle each night to remind yourself to think of your loved one. We heard from one woman whose colleague lost her son, so the woman wrote the co-worker's name on a piece of paper and kept it on her desk, reminding herself throughout the day to give her grieving office mate some "unmixed attention."

There are many versions of this type of "prayer." Franz Kafka said, "To write is to pray." St. Benedict said, "Laborare est orare," which translates, "To work is to pray." In many ways, naming something as prayer, thinking of it as a type of communion, *makes* it prayer. For some people, cooking is praying. For others, walking the dog is praying. When the mythologist Joseph Campbell was asked if he prayed, he said, "No. But every night I take a swim and then sit and have a drink with my wife."

In a time of grief, many nonreligious people find themselves in a situation—a funeral, a wake, a memorial service—where people are praying. The prayers will be filled with antiquated phrases and unfamiliar terms ("Now, which one is Yahweh?"), but instead of tuning out, listen for and appreciate the meaning and poetry beyond some of the esoteric language. Many prayers, when looked at as a text and not as religious ritual, are artful pieces of literature. If a grieving poet, psychiatrist, and anatomist collaborated to describe the experience of grief, it's doubtful they could do better than these lines from Psalm 22:

> I am poured out like water,
> and all my bones are out of joint.
> My heart has turned to wax;
> it has melted away in me.
> My strength is dried up like a potshard,
> and my tongue sticks to the roof of my mouth;
> you lay me in the dust of death.

There's a reason verses like these stay with us for centuries. Aside from their obvious connection to religious worship, their rhythms and poetic imagery and metaphors make them read almost like music, and nothing has the emotional power of music. Music is abstract enough to get through the keyhole of our subconscious mind in a way other art forms simply do not. When a song is playing, even if it's just in the car or during a TV commercial, people start involuntarily to hum or keep time, and often they begin involuntarily feeling. We have a natural connection to it.

For many people, music is the closest thing they have to a religious experience. And it's not a bad proxy. Few transcendental pleasures rank with listening to a favorite album, start to finish, eyes closed, on the couch. The writer Kurt Vonnegut, an avowed humanist and open critic of organized religion, requested that his epitaph be: "The only proof he needed of the existence of God was music." It's also interesting to note that every major religion utilizes music. It's one of the only things that connects them all. When it comes to primal expression, one could almost ask, "Which came first, the Gods or the Music?"

Very few people do not, at times, think of music as a form of spiritual expression. One look at music history shows that even the most atheistic, libertine composers wrote requiem masses, and today anyone under thirty knows that the first thing you do when you have a crush on someone is make them a "mix."

In grief, you might create your own combination of these ideas by integrating modern technology with the concept of the requiem mass. You could download music appropriate to different aspects of the person you are grieving, and, in choosing and arranging these songs, "compose" your own makeshift requiems. This may be especially helpful if you are stuck in a particularly hard phase of grief. The word "requiem," after all, means "rest."

For almost eight years Paul McCartney toyed with the idea of writing a requiem. He finished bits and pieces, but nothing that was ready for performance. When his wife of twenty-nine years, Linda, died of breast cancer in 1998, McCartney completed the piece in her memory. It was performed for the first time in November 2001 at the Sheldonian Theatre in Oxford, England. The title of the requiem is "Ecce Cora Meum." It means "behold my heart."

HONORING

How an individual chooses to honor someone they've lost is rooted in a very deep place. When honoring a lost loved one, it is the authenticity of the gesture that matters most.

One of the most touching examples of honoring in American literature is in John Steinbeck's *Grapes of Wrath*. The Joads are in mid-journey to California when the grandfather dies. It will cost forty dollars to bury him, and the family can't spare the money if they still want to make it to the West. They decide, for the good of the family, to bury him themselves, like a pauper, on the side of the road.

> Pa said softly, "Grandpa buried his pa with his own hand, done it in dignity, an' shaped the grave nice with his own shovel. That was a time when a man had the right to be buried by his own son an' a son had the right to bury his own father. Even though it's against the law I got a right to bury my own Pa."

Law or convention or anything else be damned, Pa Joad will honor his father authentically, in the way he sees fit. The family buries the old man with a note saying his name and how he died. Pa says, "He'll not be so lonesome, knowin' his name is there with 'im, not jus' a old fella lonesome underground." This is the note they leave:

> This here is William James Joad, dyed of a stroke, old old man. His fokes bured him becaws they got no money to pay for funerls. Nobody kilt him. Jus a stroke an he dyed.

It reads like an honest little unintentional poem of honoring, about which one could say Shakespeare's famous line, "Not marble, nor the gilded monuments of princes, shall outlive this powerful rhyme." It doesn't take "gilded monuments" to honor someone you love. The humblest of gestures, when done as a conscious form of honoring, can be significant.

A child, age ten, lost his grandfather. The boy was in a panic, dreading the idea of walking into a funeral home for the first time and seeing his first dead body. On the morning of the wake, one of the boy's uncles, a big athletic fellow, noticed that something was wrong with his nephew. Eventually the boy confessed what had him so rattled. Many adults in this situation would just squeal patronizingly, "Oh, I'll take you up to see grandpa," and then drag the boy up to the casket as some kind of rite of passage.

But the uncle was an emotionally intelligent guy. He suggested that his nephew stand by the door, way in the back of the large funeral parlor. He said, "Just take a quick peek from far off. If you can. If you don't want to stay, you can just go out the door right away and I'll come find you." This was wise to let the boy do everything himself—make his own decisions, honor his grandpa in his own sheepish way.

The boy did what his uncle said, got a glimpse of "what it was all about" from far off, and stayed a good while in the back of the room, observing respectfully. Thus he took his first big steps in a challenging direction. That was plenty. Relieved from the terror of thinking he *had* to do something, the boy was freer to take in other aspects of the wake. He heard his grandfather's friends go on and on about what a great fellow he was, and even met one of his grandfather's childhood girlfriends. When it was all over, the uncle told the boy, "I'm proud of how you handled that."

What constitutes honor is in the eye of the person doing the honoring.

In the case of how someone chooses to honor the physical body of someone who has died, there are those who feel that the body of the deceased is still the person, and those who do not. Some people consider a dead body sacred, and feel an urge to have some kind of interaction with the remains of their loved one. These interactions are powerful for them. If you are this kind of person and are denied an opportunity to feed this natural urge, it may cause conflict within yourself and with others.

For other people, a dead body is mere biology which should be attended to in a dignified and appropriate manner. There is no sense that the remains of a loved one are any more the person than other inanimate possessions they used in life—their car, for example. While such people go along with funerals, wakes, and burials, as far as they're concerned the person they lost is already long gone.

Regardless of which side you are on, requests involving the body of your loved one, barring anything unreasonably inappropriate, should be respected. If someone wants to send grandpa off to the taxidermist ("After all, Pappy loved hunting!"), intervene! But more often than not, though people of opposing views on this question choose ways to honor that are reasonable and defensible.

If you are the grieving person, resist being pressured in one direction or another. Your feelings about how the body should be treated are instinctual and not subject to rewiring.

C. S. Lewis, for example, loved his wife so dearly that her death sent him pacing the floors of his empty house and on to writing one of the great books on love and loss. But Lewis didn't care about his wife's mortal body. He hated the whole idea of the cemetery thing.

> I remember being rather horrified one summer morning long ago when a burly, cheerful laboring man, carrying a hoe and a watering pot came into our churchyard and, as he pulled the gate behind him, shouted over his shoulder to two friends, "See you later, I'm just going to visit Mum." He meant he was going to weed and water and generally tidy up her grave. It horrified me because this mode of sentiment, all this churchyard stuff, was and is simply hateful, even inconceivable, to me. . . . A six-by-three foot flower-bed had become Mum. That was his symbol for her, his link with her. Caring for it was visiting her.

Lewis, an impish wit even in grief, can't resist launching into a further portraiture of this man's mother. Continuing his rant, Lewis writes that the flower bed is "an obstinate, resistant, often intractable bit of reality, just as Mum in her lifetime doubtless was."

But Lewis was serious about his membership in the "body-is-not-them" category. For all the beauty (and now fame) of their love story, and its aching memorialization in *A Grief Observed*, Lewis and his wife Joy are not buried together. Joy was cremated and her ashes strewn in a public garden in Oxford. Lewis is buried at Holy Trinity Churchyard, also in Oxford. His epitaph, "Men must endure their going hence," is said to have come from a calendar that had hung in his mother's kitchen. His own gravestone was no doubt a nod of honor to *his* "mum."

As unwavering as Lewis was about the treatment of his wife's body, there are those whose feelings run just as deep in the opposite direction. Neil Santorello of Verona, Pennsylvania, lost his son, an army tank commander, in Iraq when he was killed by a roadside bomb. Upon the return of their son's remains, the Santorellos were informed by army personnel that, because of how their son was killed, his body was "unviewable." But families of servicemen killed in the line of duty have the legal right to view the remains of their loved ones. Once this right was established, Neil Santorello made this request: "I asked them to open the casket a few inches so I could reach in and take his hand."

More people nowadays side with C. S. Lewis and might find this father's action extreme at best and horrifying at worst. Still, many people have a deep longing for some type of communion with the body. Even though Suse Lowenstein's son fell from the sky onto the farm of Tundergarth below, she regrets not touching him one last time when his remains were returned to America. "I don't care that he would have been mangled, he's my son." Suse's words echo the Santorellos' comment:

> The government doesn't want you to see a serviceman in a casket, but this is my son. He is not a serviceman. You have to let his mother and I say goodbye to him.

The novelist Zadie Smith, who lost her father, was affected in a way far more common than people generally talk about.

> A nurse offered me the opportunity to see the body, which I refused. That was a mistake. It left me suspended in a bad joke in which a living man inexplicably becomes two pints of dust and everyone acts as if there were not a joke at all, but rather the most reasonable thing in the world. A body would have been usefully, concretely absurd. I would have

known—or so people say—that the thing lying there on the slab wasn't my father. As it was, I missed the death, I missed the body, I got the dust, and from these facts I tried to extrapolate a story, as writers will, but found myself, instead, in a kind of stasis.

With cremation increasingly popular, the experience Smith describes happens to people all the time. They are handed the ashes of a loved one and, like Antony referring to the mighty Julius Caesar in Shakespeare's play, can't help but feel strange seeing the person they loved "Shrunk to this little measure."

Not having seen her father's body was, as Smith said, a "mistake," and one she rectified in a way that some may find shocking. When she got the ashes home, she opened them, stuck a finger in them, and then took the finger to her mouth. Smith's case is obviously extreme, but the instinct to keep, to have, to commune, to love in the way our guts demand, is at the core of all honoring.

Of course, some instances do flummox.

When Keith Richards's father died, one could have predicted it would prompt an odd ritual from this rock star known for his hard living. (In a recent TV report, a woman whose father died at sixty-two said that his final words were, "I can't believe Keith Richards will outlive me.") Richards thought the fitting thing to do with his beloved father's ashes was to "snort them along with some cocaine." His tributary comment: "I think Pop woulda been cool with it."

Aberrant cases aside, most people's requests are not extreme. But they may be viewed as such by loved ones with opposing ideals.

While there may be more need to defend those who are compelled toward contact with the body of a deceased loved one, those who want no part of the body should also be defended.

Just as people who wish to have some interaction with the body are often vilified as "ghoulish," those who wish to stay away from "the body scene" are often wrongly considered uncaring about the person who has died.

People have a right to differences on this matter and in all things having to do with honoring those they love. In a memoir about the death of her mother, Simone de Beauvoir writes about accepting the various forms of honoring:

> It is useless to try to integrate life and death and to
> behave rationally in the presence of something that is
> not rational: each must manage as well as he can in the
> tumult of his feelings. I can understand all last wishes and
> the total absence of them: the hugging of the bones or
> the abandonment of the body of the one you love to the
> common grave. If my sister had wanted to dress Maman or
> to keep her wedding-ring I should certainly have accepted
> her reactions as willingly as my own.

Clearly this was a writer who understood grief.

In some cases the loved one who has died may leave behind specific ways for you to remember him or her. One of the most common of these is jewelry. An uncanny number of people we spoke with lifted a hand with pride to show some piece that once belonged to someone who had died. Jewelry has been a constant throughout human history and, for many, has an almost numinous power. Most jewelry is a circle—a ring, a necklace, a bracelet—and the circle is a symbol of eternity. Jewelry is also something you keep on you, a physical communion with the person who owned it.

Of course, jewelry left to you by a loved one can also pose a problem. For one thing it may be the wrong size, or a style that's ill-suited to you. If you're a guy who works on Wall Street and your uncle from Arizona leaves you a ring that looks like a turquoise meteorite, touched as you might be, you're not about to wear it to the next staff meeting. But people find creative ways to reconfigure jewelry into more usable forms. They will wear a ring that's too small on a chain, as a pendant. Or be like the fellow who showed us a cigarette lighter encrusted with small diamonds from a bracelet of his deceased mom's.

One of the nicest ways of honoring we heard about came from the life of Shakespeare—and involved jewelry. From the moment of his birth, Shakespeare lived in a grief-drenched era, a time in which the plague was particularly virulent. The year he was born, of sixty-three infants christened in Stratford, sixty died. That's quite a way to get started, and for all his life Shakespeare was well acquainted with grief. By age thirty-seven he'd lost both his father and his son.

In his last will and testament, Shakespeare set aside money for some of his companions to buy rings to commemorate their relationship. To his best friends, including Richard Burbage, the first actor to play Hamlet, Shakespeare left *"26 shillings, 8 pence a peece to buy them Rings"* in celebration of their friendship.

This seems a fine and gracious thing to do: to leave or be left money for a piece of jewelry to commemorate someone who has died. Whether the sum is enough to shop on Rodeo Drive or merely to buy a gewgaw from an arts and crafts fair in Portland, it makes no difference. The gesture is meant to turn the unique story of your relationship into a lasting symbol of love, which is the essence of honoring.

MEANING

"I am someone who has been glued back together."

These words, a memorial tribute from the obituary page of a New York newspaper, were written by a loved one in honor of the second anniversary of someone's death. This is the best metaphor we could find to describe grief, a subject so visceral that people almost always use metaphors when discussing it. If you are grieving, you are broken. Either someone's illness and death has chipped away at you piece by piece, or a sudden tragedy has slammed you apart.

But broken is not dead. Your loved one has died, you haven't.

The trajectory of any grief begins with a pile of pieces and concludes with you coming to terms with what the loved one meant to you. A good way to end up would be like the man who said about his deceased wife: "A man who has nothing left in this world still may know bliss, be it only for a brief moment, in the contemplation of his beloved."

Someone struggling with grief might wish to respond, "Yeah, right, I'll just sit here and contemplate my fucking beloved. Thanks Buddy." But the man who was able to "know bliss" was Viktor Frankl, the psychotherapist whose wife and parents were killed in Auschwitz. Whatever hell you may be going through, chances are Frankl had it worse. And his epiphany about "contemplating his beloved" did not come in later life; it occurred when he was in a concentration camp. In fact the next thing he writes is:

> In front of me a man stumbled and those following him fell on top of him. The guard rushed over and used his whip on them all. Thus my thoughts were interrupted. . .

Frankl went on to develop a form of psychoanalysis he called logotheraphy, in which patients learn to search for meaning in an awful situation. Frankl's theory is that when everything has crumbled, it is still possible to put the fragments back together into something that has meaning enough to sustain you, or at least to keep you from decimation.

This approach is helpful to people in grief for two reasons. First, "meaning" is about truth. It promises no false dawns and doesn't take off into its own happy ending. Meaning asks only that you look at what you *had* and what you now *have*, and recognize your situation for what it is.

Second, the human brain is prewired to find meaning. Grief concepts like "letting go," or "closure," or "acceptance" don't work because they run contrary to this wiring. They are virtuous psychological contortions, unsustainable because they're unnatural. But finding meaning is very natural for people. We do it all the time. It's one of the more useful tools of personhood available to us. Grief and death aside, we use meaning to put together the small pieces of life in general. So what if your kid hits a homer in Little League? He'll probably never play in the pros. So what if your parents reach their fiftieth wedding anniversary? Fifty is just a number, and they're hardly lovebirds any more. And who cares about the old Zippo your grandfather gave you? It probably cost him two bucks when he bought it, and you don't even smoke.

The only reason any of these things matter is because of *meaning*. We choose to see meaning in things and people, and that's what makes them ours.

When a loved one dies, you are left only with meaning. In whatever form you recognize it, that meaning is all you have to flesh out what Billy Collins calls the "shape of air walking in their place."

The problem is, when you are in grief, *meaning* slams head on into *want*. Meaning be damned, you *want* the person back. You want him! You want her! This yearning can make it hard to settle for a conceptual idea of the loved one who has died—

however ennobling—when what you really want is to be able to take that person to a movie and then out for sushi. Philosophy rarely trumps dinner, and the "idea" is never as good as the here and now. When Woody Allen was told that after his death he would live on in his work, he said, "I would prefer to live on in my apartment."

Even the writers we turn to again and again in this book, people whose jobs, and fame, stem from their ability to find and express meaning, fall short in this regard. Like everyone else, they exist between meaning and want.

Many people were surprised by *The Year of Magical Thinking*. Joan Didion is a writer known for her blunt style and unwavering common sense. The idea that she could succumb to "magical thinking" seemed unfathomable. "Magical thinking" is a term used to describe a stream of thought that is casual and non-scientific, what some would call superstition. In grief you may be fully aware that your thoughts are illogical, but this awareness doesn't prevent the thoughts from coming. When Didion writes about poring over her dead husband's medical records in search of the overlooked detail "they might still be able to fix," or how, when considering the time difference between coasts, she wonders if his death "had also happened in Los Angeles," it's a line of magical thought surprisingly unlike her. The novelist Mona Simpson referred to Didion as "the writer one would think *least* subject to magical thinking." When the interviewer Charlie Rose said how surprised he was that a powerhouse journalist like Didion could fall into magical thinking, she replied, "Well, there it is. We're all human after all." She wanted her husband back.

As noted earlier, when C. S. Lewis originally wrote *A Grief Observed*, he did so under a pseudonym. The book was published in the year after his wife's death. Lewis's friends felt he was still in such a bad way that they began recommending the book to *him*! As honestly as Lewis expressed his grief in that book, his want for his wife remained so obvious that those closest to him thought he could benefit from "this new book I heard about by N. W. Clerk . . ."

And finally, a physician who wrote a book called *How We Die* is clearly someone who has accepted the fact that biology forces us to let go. Yet Sherwin Nuland had trouble relinquishing his own "want" when it came to the illness and eventual death of his brother Harvey.

Nuland was the primary adviser during Harvey's treatment for intestinal cancer. Against his better instincts as a physician, he encouraged his brother to go forward with a "Hail Mary" treatment even though he "knew about the toxicity of experimental drugs." Nuland admits, "I let my instincts as a brother overwhelm my judgment as a surgeon who has spent his career treating people with lethal diseases." He couldn't let go. His want was too strong. Nuland concludes:

> Harvey paid a high price for the unfulfilled promise of hope. I had offered him the opportunity to try the impossible, though I knew the trying would be bought at the expense of major suffering. Where my own brother was concerned, I had forgotten, or at least forsaken, the lessons learned from decades of experience.

"Well, there it is. We're all human after all."
Even when people screw up, when want outweighs meaning—when Didion can't stop her magical thinking, when Lewis won't learn the lessons in his own book, when Nuland can't let go of his brother, or when you are grieving and think you're going crazy—it's because love can make people act that way. In a strange way, grief makes us all fools for love. Human beings are stuck somewhere in a twilight zone between "want" and

"meaning." Lewis captures the cosmic comedy of this paradox and muses on the incongruity of our Creator to

> make an organism which is also a spirit; to make that terrible oxymoron, a "spiritual animal." To take a poor primate, a beast with nerve-endings all over it, a creature with a stomach that wants to be filled, a breeding animal that wants its mate, and say, "Now get on with it. Become a god."

In times of grief, our "God self" and our "animal self" have a difficult time striking a balance.

A nine-year-old boy, an only child, lost his mother to a cancer she had fought for years. The mother died in a hospital a few blocks from the family's home, so the boy and his father would routinely pass it on their way to and fro. Every time they did, the boy would react. He'd wince, scowl, or make a glum comment about the building. This went on for a while, until the father thought something should be done.

The next time it happened, the father pulled into the hospital parking lot. He took his son out of the car, held his hand, and faced the front entrance. He said, "The worst day of my life happened in that building. Because that's where your mom died. But the *best* day of my life happened in that building. Because that's where you were born." The father and son then went into the hospital's maternity ward and spent some time at the nursery window looking at newborns.

Meaning does for a grieving person what this father did for his son. Just as he took his child by the hand, walked him into the "bad place," and showed him that death *and* birth are *both* part of a hospital, "meaning" takes grieving people by the hand, walks them into the bad place (usually kicking and screaming), and shows them that we get both *grief* and *joy* in this world, and that the two are interconnected.

C. S. Lewis was a lifelong bachelor until, quite late in life, he met and married Joy Davidson, an American woman with two young sons. Before ever meeting her, Lewis wrote a book on spirituality entitled *Surprised by Joy*, so after the real Joy walked into his life, there was no end to the "surprised by Joy, indeed" jokes among his friends. And since Davidson turned out to be quite a spitfire, and every bit the commonsense equal to Lewis's scholarly intellect, it was as if the heavens had smiled on the whole enterprise.

But then her cancer came. It was terminal, and they both knew it. The height of their happiness together would make for a hard fall into grief when Joy died, as they knew she would.

The film *Shadowlands* depicts the whole story and stars Anthony Hopkins and Debra Winger (both so wonderful in it). In the film is a scene during the time that can happen for a gravely ill person, when Joy was feeling spry, even merry for a while before her final decline. We heard many stories about this phenomenon, a kind of victory lap around the goodness of life that some people experience before dying.

During this time for Joy, the two of them take a vacation. It's an idyllic trip, but she can't help but talk about "later." While afraid of what's to come, she says, "The pain then is part of the happiness now. That's the deal."

That is the deal. Grief and joy are both part of hospitals, relationships, and life. One is payment for the other. Grief is a bill you get for having loved the person you've lost. Grief hurts in direct proportion to how joyous that love was. The lot of every grieving person is to be, in the words of Emily Dickinson, "Enlightened to a larger pain/ By contrast with the love."

The pain that you are "enlightened to" may make you wonder whether having your loved one for the time you did was all worth it. Would there have been less pain if there had been less love? After Mel Brooks lost his wife, Anne Bancroft, he said to a friend, "Maybe I should have stayed married to my first wife. Losing her wouldn't have been so painful." Many people express such feelings. The grief bill they get after someone dies is a shocker.

But while your loved one may be gone, your love for that person is not. The playwright Robert Anderson said, "Death ends a life, but it doesn't end a relationship." You still have a relationship with your loved one in your feelings, thoughts, memories, and love for that person. For some, this so-called relationship, like all relationships, can be a bit dysfunctional. One woman took out this "in memoriam" ad for her husband: "To My Beloved. I have been in misery every day since you died. Not one happy moment." This appeared in 2005, but the man died in 1964. Forty-one years of unmitigated misery? (One can imagine the children drawing straws to see who gets mom for the holidays.)

For others, the relationship with the person who has died can be more vivid and active. Douglas Hofstadter is a Pulitzer Prize–winning author and professor of cognitive science at Indiana University. In 1993 he lost his wife suddenly to a brain tumor and was left with their two children, ages five and two.

Hofstadter recently wrote a book called *I Am a Strange Loop*, in which he advances a theory about his wife's soul. He's a scientist, so he makes it clear that he uses the word "soul" not in a religious way but because he feels it "most evocatively suggests the deep mystery of first-person existence that any philosophically inclined person must wonder about many times during their life." He speaks about his late wife as "a detailed, elaborate pattern that exists very clearly in one's brain." He claims that "when a person dies, the original is no longer around. But there are other versions of it in other people's brains." He refers to these pieces of a person that embed themselves in their loved ones' brains as "soul-shards."

Being a scientist, when Hofstadter went public with this theory of consciousness he got plenty of flack. It's odd to have someone in such an unremittingly rational field talk publicly in such a touchingly speculative way. One interviewer pressed him: "You make it sound as if a soul can be Xeroxed." But Hofstadter explained that a soul-shard is not an "exact copy" but rather more "coarse-grained and approximate. Lower resolution." He concludes, "My wife and I became so intimately engaged that her essence has imported into my brain."

The more one studies grief, the less far-fetched it seems to think of each person as an "elaborate pattern" that does become "embedded" in the minds and hearts of those he or she loves. This is perhaps why stories about grief are never only depressing but often life affirming. Aspects of them are sad, yes, but they tell us so much about how unique a life was, how distinct a love was, the depths to which human beings can feel, that they are often inspiring and invigorating. Stories of the dead bring them to life for us. Even if they were strangers. Consider, for example, the words of this anonymous obituary:

> My mother was the kind of woman who could walk into a revolving door behind you and come out first.

You've never met this woman or her son who wrote the obituary; you have no information about her whatsoever. But in less than twenty words you can't help but know her in a flash, can't help but perceive a "pattern," can't help but have a few of her soul-shards embed themselves in your brain. And this is without ever laying eyes on the woman. Imagine how many soul-shards her son has, how many pixels of meaning he has available to build on.

Now imagine how many soul-shards the person you lost has left behind for you to work with. Probably a lot. Going forward with your life will mean taking those fragments and gathering them into a version of loving the person that you can live with—and even someday come to enjoy. The alternative is that the loved one you lost will be nothing more for you than a tragedy, a bill for love, a "shape of air," a grief.

This is the challenge of grief: to take the mess of pieces you fell into upon your loved one's death and glue yourself together into something approaching "whole." Broken, yes. Reglued, yes. But a version of whole nonetheless. This is the trajectory of grief, moving from someone's death back into living your life again. This is the arc every griever travels. And what a trip it is—one that only a poet like Auden could capture. In his poem "The More Loving One," he describes how it feels to be the one left behind, with nothing but your love for someone who has died. It begins with the abandoned speaker angry and bitter and shouting to the sky: "Looking up at the stars, I know quite well/ That, for all they care, I can go to hell." But it ends with what seems like a glimmer of going on—not closure or peace, just going on.

> Were all stars to disappear or die,
> I should learn to look at an empty sky
> And feel its total dark sublime,
> Though this might take me a little time.

It does take time. But many grieving people say that even in the "dark" of this time, something in you settles. There is an awareness of deep gratitude—that you had the person for as long as you did. And for many there is pride—that your names appear together in the book of the universe and that somewhere it is written: he or she was yours—*your* parent, *your* child, *your* sibling, *your* love, *your* boon companion. And, death be damned, nothing can change that.

This is, finally, all you are left with: what you *meant* to someone and what she or he *meant* to you. The hope is that, in the fullness of time, meaning wins out over grief. While now this may seem like a tall order, ask yourself this question: If there were a way to erase all the grief you feel, but it would mean also erasing the person from having ever been in your life, would you sign on to such a deal? We asked a number of people this question and never found anyone who would. Maybe this realization—that loving the person you lost was worth it, *is* worth it—maybe this is the place to begin.

ACKNOWLEDGMENTS

Excerpt from "Distressed Haiku" from *The Painted Bed: Poems by Donald Hall*. Copyright © 2002 by Donald Hall. Reprinted by permission of Houghton Mifflin Publishing Company. All rights reserved.

Mary Oliver, from *Thirst*. Copyright © 2007 by Mary Oliver. Reprinted by permission of Beacon Press.

"Obituaries," from *Nine Horses* by Billy Collins, copyright © 2002 by Billy Collins. Used by permission of Random House, Inc.

Excerpt from "Kill the Day" from *The Painted Bed: Poems by Donald Hall*. Copyright © 2002 by Donald Hall. Reprinted by permission of Houghton Mifflin Publishing Company. All rights reserved.

Excerpt from "Funeral Blues," copyright © 1940 and renewed 1968 by W. H. Auden, from *Collected Poems of W. H. Auden* by W. H. Auden. Used by permission of Random House, Inc.

Karen Swenson, "A Sense of Direction" from *A Daughter's Latitude: New & Selected*. Copyright © 1999 by Karen Swenson.

INDEX

A NOTE ON THE AUTHORS

Ron Marasco is a professor in the College of Communication and Fine Arts at Loyola Marymount University, in Los Angeles. He has a PhD from UCLA. His first book, *Notes to an Actor*, was named by the American Library Association as an "Outstanding Academic Book of 2008." For the past five years he has taught a very popular undergraduate course on the subject of grief using film, theatre, literature, and oral history as a way to study this, often intimidating, subject. He has acted extensively on TV—in everything from *Lost* to *West Wing* to *Entourage*—and appeared opposite screen legend Kirk Douglas in the movie *Illusion*, for which he also wrote the screenplay.

Brian Shuff is a writer from Mesa, Arizona, who now lives in Los Angeles where he is at work completing a book of short stories. His mother died when he was eight years old, giving him a lifelong interest in the subject of grief. Along with Ron Marasco he has written a screenplay based on Louise Hay's groundbreaking book *You Can Heal Your Life* that will premiere in 2011. He and Marasco are also working on a dramatic adaptation of John McNulty's short-story collection, *This Place on Third Avenue*.